■SCHOLASTIC

The PreK–2 Writing Classroom

Growing Confident Writers

Jane Hansen, Robyn Davis, Jenesse Evertson,

Tena Freeman, Dorothy Suskind, Holly Tower

D1504906

New York • Toronto • London • Auckland • Sydney
Mexico City • New Delhi • Hong Kong • Buenos Aires

Teaching Resources

● ● ● ●

Scholastic grants teachers permission to photocopy the reproducible pages from this book for classroom use. No other part of this publication may be reproduced in whole or in part, or stored in a retrieval system, or transmitted in any form or by any means, electronic, mechanical, photocopying, recording, or otherwise, without permission of the publisher. For information regarding permission, write to Scholastic Inc., 557 Broadway, New York, NY 10012.

Cover Design and Photograph: Maria Lilja
Interior Design: Sarah Morrow
Editor: Lois Bridges
Production/Copy Editor: Danny Miller

Copyright © 2010 by Jane Hansen
All rights reserved. Published by Scholastic Inc.
Printed in the U.S.A.
ISBN: 978-0-545-20868-0

2   3   4   5   6   7   8   9   10   40   17   16   15   14   13   12   11

CONTENTS

Our Young Writers Set Us Straight

Do you know how to turn a square into a grown-up?

Or how to turn a piece of writing about monster trucks into a piece of writing about autumn?

Or even how to put a giant troll to sleep?

When our young children write, we are often surprised by what their words tell us. We marvel at their big ideas, such as how to lull a troll into slumber, as well as how they place those ideas onto paper—how they learn to create spaces between words, draw, make letters, and use periods.

The magnitude of what our writers are learning to do amazes us. They are learning an entirely new form of communication in such a relatively small amount of time! When we view monster trucks and squares from *their* viewpoint, we learn that, as professionals, sometimes we need to be set straight.

Six of us—a mix of teachers currently in the classroom, former teachers, and former teachers now at universities researching children—spent a few years studying young writers in their classrooms and learned what the children did when they wrote across the curriculum and what that means for the teaching of writing. As we watched the children write and then wrote snapshots about them, these snapshots pushed us to look at young children's writing in new ways.

Quandra, a prekindergarten writer, was one of the first children to step in front of us and open our eyes wide!

A Prekindergarten Writer

A small group of prekindergarten writers in Robyn Davis's classroom sit together on the rug. She has laid out letter cards, and the children are eying them, waiting for their turn to pull the one corresponding to the first letter in their name. Because they are only four and because many of them have had few opportunities to interact with text prior to these early days of pre-K, the children sometimes choose a card with a letter that does not begin their name. Miss Robyn, as she is known by her students, patiently asks them to look again and give it another go. When it is Quandra's turn to choose her letter, she doesn't move. Miss Robyn notices that the 'Q' is not among the other letters. She looks at Quandra enquiringly. Quandra lifts herself from the floor—she's been sitting on the 'Q' the whole time! "Ain't nobody be messin' with my 'Q,'" she says adamantly, "NOBODY!"

On another day, when Quandra had painted at the easel, Miss Robyn moved her painting aside so another child could paint. In doing so, Miss Robyn carefully printed Quandra's name in the corner of her painting, but when Quandra saw what Miss Robyn had done, she screamed, "You write my name, it no be my name!"

Quandra can write her own Q, and nobody else is to mess with it, including Miss Robyn, who learned right then and there to stop writing the children's names. They learn to write them to identify their own paintings and writing—where their names count. A Q is enough. No one else's signature is a Q.

These very young children feel *strongly* about text that is connected to them.

Writing is powerful.

Writing is personal.

Entering this new world of print is important to young children but, of course, they encounter the challenges that accompany any exploration of new territory. What do they do then?

A Five-year-old At-home Writer

Five-year-old Joe, the son of Jenesse Evertson, sits at the little table in her home office, sorting through a stack of photos from an initial visit to England, before it became his home. "'Member these soldiers?" he asks his mum. She does.

"They were big—and scary!" They had seen the Queen's Guard practicing for an upcoming public procession on the green in Windsor, and in all their regalia and upon their shiny black horses, they cut imposing figures indeed.

"Would you like to write about that?" Jenesse asks her son. He slowly nods his head. The dilemma is this: he would *like* to write, but writing is difficult for him. He can't remember what he writes. Ever. Unless he rereads the entry for many, many days in a row. Joe says he is the only boy in his class who can't read anything—"Not even my own writing!"

But on this day, Joe decides that this particular experience is worth the effort. So, he puts his pencil to the paper and writes: THE SLJRS Wr TLL and SCARE. He stares and stares at this writing for a minute. Then, he very meticulously begins covering the word "scary" with spikes. Next, he erases the word "tall" and remakes it with letters as big as can fit in the space. "I'll remember this now," he says with a grin of satisfaction.

Over the next few weeks, Joe expands on these initial explorations. He underlines the word *green* with green crayon and shades the word *dark* with his pencil. He makes little marks next to other words that serve as mnemonic devices for remembering them. Those triggers enable him to remember the entire drafts.

Joe created a strategy to help turn writing from a meaningless activity to a meaningful one! Will it always work? Probably not, but for the moment, Joe proceeds with confidence. Importantly, he now knows that he can push himself forward as a writer.

What This May Mean for Your Classroom

You want your young writers to feel strongly about their experiences with print. Your moments with them cause you to pause, to learn. As teachers, however, there is much in your school day that causes you to pause: conflicts between students, unannounced fire drills, rain, new textbook adoptions, curricular requirements, and many children speaking many languages in one space.

Sometimes it takes a great deal of determination to zero in on children while they write so you do not miss out on the marvelous things they do with marker in hand. When you pause and take a close look at them, you wonder, "What does this mean for my teaching? Because I sat beside a little girl when she tried to draw her first person, what do I do to capitalize on that significant moment?"

Your questions are similar to those of the teachers you will read about in the following chapters.

The Teachers in This Book

Like their students, the teachers profiled in this book are nothing if not resourceful! Robyn Davis, Sue Harris, Elaine O'Connor, and Tena Freeman learned to be so when it came to their young writers. Sue Harris, for one, found herself in the midst of a district-mandated two-hour literacy block that did *not* provide time for writing. Having seen in previous years, however, what her young writers could do, gave Sue pause; she valued their writing and, like the other teachers, placed priority on squeezing in time for it.

So what do these teachers do when they teach writing?

They all organize their writing time a bit differently, to be sure. But they have these things in common:

- They begin their writing time on the first day of school, even in Miss Robyn's prekindergarten.

- They create time for writing at least four days a week.

- They demonstrate what writers do by creating their own drafts in front of the children and talking about each writing step they take and why.

- They talk about the "author's craft" as they read aloud from children's literature.

- They take their time with a topic or writing feature they want to demonstrate. First-grade teacher Elaine O'Connor may demonstrate an aspect of writing for a week, second-grade teacher Tena Freeman for longer.

- They include a regular, if not daily, sharing time.

- They interact with their young writers throughout the writing time.

In this book, we use the term "writing workshop" to refer to the writing time these teachers create for their young students. They use that term as well, but rather than strictly adhering to any particular prescription for a "writing workshop," these teachers think carefully about the principles behind the surface features of their writing workshops and stay true them. As you will see, each teacher's writing workshop looks a bit different. This is because each classroom community is different, each school is different, and each teacher is different.

But they all recognize the huge importance in the little things their young writers do. And that sets them straight.

The University Researchers in This Book

The university researchers in this book—Jenesse Evertson, Holly Tower, Dorothy Suskind, and Jane Hansen—were not teachers at the time they studied the young writers mentioned in the book. Jane is a university professor and the others were doctoral students. All of them had been teachers, however, and taught in different decades, in different areas of the United States, in other countries, within different grade levels, and in specialist roles. For this project, they each spent two mornings or afternoons a week for at least a year in one of the classrooms, interacting with the children, conducting demonstrations, and observing what the young writers did as they wrote.

About This Book

In the following chapters, the six authors outline the kinds of writing instruction that help children become engaged, resourceful, confident writers.

Each chapter is framed around a the following features:

- Snapshots of Students

- What These Writers Can Do: Strengths and Breakthroughs

- What the Teachers Do

- Writer-Friendly Classroom Features

- What This May Mean for Your Classroom

- Closing Thoughts

Each chapter opens with snapshots of children as they write, our reflections on the snapshots, and descriptions of the teachers' instructional decisions that preceded and/or followed the events highlighted in the snapshot. "What the Teachers Do" is particularly important. The teachers' decisions are based on what they have seen and heard their children do as writers, and it's these informed observations that enable the teachers to respond to their students in ways that move their young writers forward on their developmental journey toward more conventional writing.

So, onward! Elaine O'Connor always encourages her first-grade students to "Try to write something that no one else will," and we have followed her wise guidance in our book. Now, we invite you to read as no one else will. We hope that in the following pages you discover something new and important about developing writers and the teaching of writing that will inform your work with your young writers.

And, in case you're still wondering, "How do you turn a square into a grown-up?" read Chapter 1 and find out!

CHAPTER 1

We Encourage Our Writers to Draw

In order to be writers, children must know they have information to convey, and they must be able to figure out a way to accomplish that feat. When some young children write across the curriculum, they convey their information with both drawing and print. Very young writers, however, who do not yet use print, often draw and redraw as their way to explore the possibilities of using paper to say something important.

Snapshot of Charles
A First-Grade Writer

It is writing workshop time in this first-grade classroom, and the children have become fully accustomed to the writing routine. On Tuesdays and Thursdays they write on topics their teacher, Elaine O'Connor, chooses; on Mondays and Wednesdays the young writers write on topics of their own choice.

Today is Tuesday and, as we join the class, Ms. O'Connor begins the writing workshop with a mini-lesson on writing about math.

Charles, sitting on the floor in the cluster of children, watches and listens closely to his teacher. The class is studying shapes, and Ms. O'Connor wants them to write about two shapes today.

"Who can think of two shapes?"

"A circle and a rectangle!"

"Yes! How are they the same or different?" asks Ms. O'Connor.

"A circle goes like this and a rectangle like this," shows the child with his hands. Charles watches.

"Yes, let's talk about that," responds Ms. O'Connor, and she and the class discuss the similarities and differences.

Then Ms. O'Connor asks, "How about an oval and a circle? Who can tell us how they are the same or different?"

"The oval is long," says someone, and they discuss this. Charles listens.

Now it is time for the children to write, and Ms. O'Connor says, "When you write today, you will choose two shapes and write about how they are the same or different."

Then Ms. O'Connor adds her daily note of encouragement: *"Try to write something no one else will write."*

The children hurry to their tables, but Charles walks slowly. He sits for a bit, looks out the window, writes his name on his paper, and then studies his pencil. He is being himself. A thinker.

Then he writes, and Jane Hansen, the researcher in the classroom, watches him from afar as she confers with children at another table. When she eventually stops beside Charles, he excitedly reads to her:

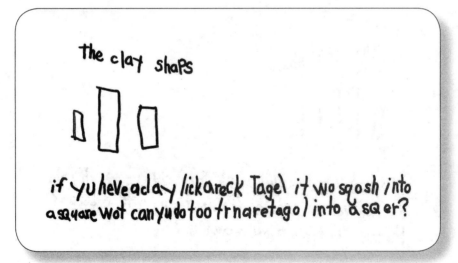

"If you have a clay like a rectangle it would squish into
a square. What can you do to turn a rectangle into a square?"

Then, to Mrs. Hansen's surprise, Charles flips his paper and shows the answer to his question on the back:

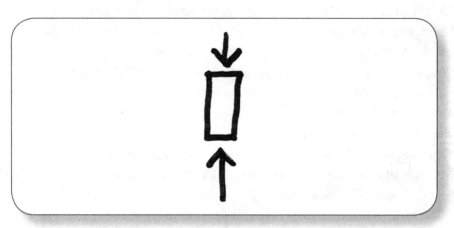

For days Charles has been reading riddles, loves them, and is obviously trying his hand at one! Plus, of course, he is working on his writing assignment (Hansen, 2005). And, importantly, he is honoring his teacher's mantra: He is writing something no one else is writing. No one else is creating a riddle.

Charles, however, is not finished. He looks Mrs. Hansen in the eye, and says, "When you come back, I'll have something else." She takes that as a cue to leave.

Several minutes later she returns, and Charles reads his new riddle to her:

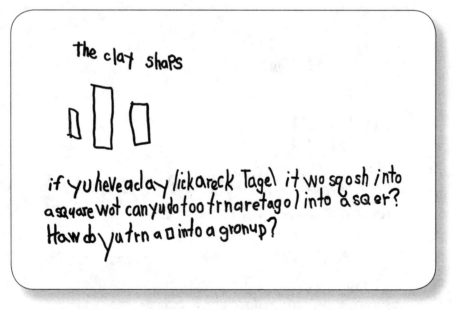

"How do you turn a square into a grown-up?"

Before Mrs. Hansen can possibly try to answer, Charles flips his paper, and the two of them enjoy his surprising answer!

"Turn it into a rectangle."

What This Writer Can Do: Strengths and Breakthroughs

- Charles can convey mathematical information in both print and drawing. This is an important feature of mathematical writing. In math texts we see a combination of words and graphics of various kinds. It is important for the children to realize that a combination of forms of writing is the authentic manner in which writers convey mathematical information.

- Charles can integrate his print and visuals. He did not separate them, as we often see in children's writing. In other words, the drawing is not on the top of a sheet of paper, with the text written below. No, Charles used one continuous writing process in which he conveyed what he wanted to say by naturally moving back and forth between print and drawing.

- Charles can write about his math in an innovative way—he creates riddles. His first-grade teacher did not need to require her writers to use particular writing formulas when they wrote in math. Throughout the entire year, they studied, read, and enjoyed many forms of print and learned to convey their content in ways that worked for them. To choose to write mathematical information in the form of riddles is certainly an effective way for a first-grade child to experiment with writing and to convey his mathematical knowledge. Riddles can approach any topic in the world—including square adults who may stretch out of their squares some day.

A Prekindergarten Writer

Four-year-old Tessa sits among her classmates in her prekindergarten classroom, quietly writing on her own, while her tablemates keep up a steady stream of chatter with one another as they write (Kissel, 2008a).

During the first several weeks of school, Tessa draws train tracks each day, and refers to them as "choo-choo trains."

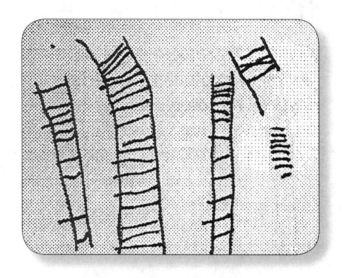

Tessa's choo-choo trains

Day after day she creates similar train tracks. She explains that they run behind her house, and her father often comes home on the train.

During October, the class studies the natural changes in the world around them, focusing on the harvest. Their teacher, Miss Robyn, reads several nonfiction and fiction books about apples to them, they take a trip to an orchard, and Miss Robyn writes about apples in her own writing at an easel as the children interact with her.

After several days of their study, Tessa once again begins her writing by creating her familiar image. Then, she picks up a red marker and places a round dot at the bottom of each track. Next, she makes shapes at the bottom of her page with a purple marker, and fills in the shapes with red:

"I write choo-choo tracks and red apples," she proudly exclaims!

What This Writer Can Do: Strengths and Breakthroughs

- Tessa knows the essence of writing. In prekindergarten, with writing utensils available to her for the first time in her life, she conveys her thoughts in her own way. Not yet sure of how to draw people, Tessa figures out an effective means by which to share her thoughts with her tablemates, her classmates, her teacher, and the researcher in her classroom.

- Tessa explores one idea for several days: Her dad arrives on these train tracks. Similar to some professional authors, she repeatedly writes about one topic. Her dad is on her mind, and she is in a strange place during these beginning days of prekindergarten. Tessa has never left home or her family for an extended

(continued on next page)

period of time, and her days in this prekindergarten classroom worry her. When will she see her dad again? Does he know where she is?

- Tessa steps into the content of the classroom! In a way that surprises all of us, Tessa writes about apples. Writing about their units of study is not required for these very new writers, but Tessa and her classmates have studied apples for days, and she feels comfortable trying to draw/write about them. Tessa, importantly, keeps her dad in her writing. He can share a space with the apples of his daughter's new life. Tessa has brought together her two worlds—her old world of home and her new world of school. This was a big day for this young child!

What the Teachers Do

Charles's first-grade teacher gives her writers flexibility about when to draw within the creation of a piece of writing.

Ms. O'Connor provides this flexibility in order to encourage greater success among her young writers. On the day Charles wrote about rectangles and squares, she told them to compare and contrast any two shapes of their choice, and to "try to write something no one else will write."

Ms. O'Connor does not tell her writers when to draw. They may draw before or after they place print on their papers, or they may interweave their use of print and drawing, as Charles did on this particular day. Writing is a process that includes drawing. The various aspects of writing fit together differently for various children on any given day, depending on the way a child wants to create the message he or she has decided to convey.

The children in Ms. O'Connor's first-grade class understand that when it is time to write, their teacher expects them to use print and drawing in whatever ways further their purposes.

In addition, Ms. O'Connor:

- circulates among the children while they write.

- provides time every day for her first graders to read books of their choice. Of course, they develop favorites and often use them for ideas when they write.

- teaches her writers to use the sounding-out skills they are learning in reading. At the same time, she teaches them that writing is not spelling. If Charles had asked, "Ms. O'Connor, how do you spell *turn*?" she would simply have reminded him, "You can do what we have practiced. Say the word very slowly and write the sounds you hear. Let me hear you start to do that."

- works with the children to create a Word Wall as they learn new sight words; Charles could have copied *like* from it, but he was too engrossed in his writing to let the use of the word wall interrupt him.

- displays words for the curriculum-area studies on posters. Charles could have copied *rectangle* but, again, he was too immersed in the creation of his riddles to stop and copy that long word.

- knows it would not be wise to interrupt her writers' engagement to remind them to copy words. All of her writers gradually learn to write their words in a more conventional manner.

Tessa's prekindergarten teacher understands that the essence of writing is the urge to say something. She recognizes that her young writers can satisfy this urge by drawing. For them, drawing is writing.

Robyn Davis's prekindergarten children come to school each day expecting time to write. Their young minds have been full of thoughts for years!

At the beginning of the year, all of them write in the form of drawings.

Some of her very young writers have never used crayons and markers, and the making of a mark is a new, amazing experience; they spend many days experimenting with these new tools.

Every day, while they write, Miss Robyn moves among the tables of busy writers, listening and watching. As they finish she says to each one, "Please tell me what you wrote about today." At first, some of them have no answer—they are making marks. Gradually, they realize that writing says something and they start to become intentional. Their writing takes on recognizable shapes.

For some of them, such as Tessa, they seemingly repeat a similar pattern for days, an exploration Miss Robyn has learned is worthwhile. Ashley Bryan, a noted children's illustrator, confirms the importance of Tessa's repetitions. He taught for many years, and his goal was to "create a situation in which the children would not be dependent upon me but would rather come with a tremendous sense of excitement about whatever it was that they had to offer.

I remember one child who, day after day, painted columns of star-like forms in different colors. The other children said to him, 'You're always painting stars!' and the child kept on painting stars. I never said to him, 'You've already done that,' which so often happens to a child. You let the child go to the limit, the exhaustion of possibility . . . Any motif is absolutely endless in its possibilities of exploration, and you don't know beforehand how far a child might like to go with an idea" (Marcus, 2002, pp. 26–27).

Miss Robyn, in recognizing drawing as a way to convey meaning, sees her students as writers on Day 1. And they see themselves as such. None of the children say they can't write. They all have ideas in their heads that they would like to transpose onto paper. Importantly, Miss Robyn knows her young children have those ideas on their minds. Thus, they can write!

In addition:

- Miss Robyn wants to expand her children's repertoire, so she opens their daily writing workshop by reading good children's literature aloud.

- As she reads to the children, they interact with her, gaining the oral language practice they need.

- Over a period of time, Miss Robyn rereads a book many times, and the children begin to read along with her.

- Sometimes the children use ideas from children's literature in their writing.

- Also, Miss Robyn creates her own piece of writing each day at an easel as a demonstration lesson. Typically, a small handful of children borrow her idea and use it in their own writing.

Writer-Friendly Classroom Features

Charles's First-Grade Classroom

If you had walked into Charles's first-grade classroom on the day he created his riddles, you would have found yourself amid round tables. The children spend their days at these tables—Ms. O'Connor requested tables rather than desks. Six children can fit at a table, but there are usually four at each. A basket of crayons and a can of pencils sit at the center of each table.

The children, when they leave Ms. O'Connor's lesson to go write, can sit wherever they want. They do not always sit in the same place or with the same people. You see the children deciding where to sit as part of what they do when they settle in to write. This is important, overall, as some of them know they want to sit near certain children.

On this particular day, one child wants to write about ovals and circles. He doesn't know how to draw an oval so he seeks someone who knows how and intentionally sits beside that person.

Before long, all the children are writing, which means you see some of them drawing before they create print, some after, and some drawing throughout.

Tessa's Prekindergarten Classroom

If you had entered Tessa's prekindergarten classroom on the day she placed apples under her train tracks, you would have heard Miss Robyn open their writing workshop by reading nonfiction aloud to the children. The children enjoy this read-aloud time and excitedly interact with Miss Robyn.

Then Miss Robyn rises, stands at the easel beside her, and with marker in hand, asks, "What am I going to do?" "Write your name!" they all chorus, and she writes: *Miss Robyn.*

Then she creates her piece of writing for this day—about apples. As she does so, the children interact with her, giving her ideas. "How many apples do you think I should pick?" "Two." "Three." "Four!"

The children, after Miss Robyn finishes her writing, each tell the class what they intend to write about. As they do, they go off, one by one, to what have become their usual spots at certain tables, even though they do not have assigned seats. As they fit themselves onto the benches, they start to dig around in the tray of tools, deciding what they want to use. Some of them choose one tool, and some gather several.

As they begin, a few of them print a letter or two to represent their names, the task Miss Robyn is teaching them within the context of their writing. That is where their names count, as we learned from Quandra in the Introduction. The children love the creations they produce each day. Before long Tessa will either start to write her name or Miss Robyn will encourage her to do so.

After the children write their names, they start to chatter about what they are going to write. As they begin their creations, some children start to draw shapes and others draw recognizable scenes. At the beginning of the year, almost all the prekindergarten children write about their out-of-school lives, where their thoughts seem to be centered. Gradually, as school gains in importance, they add school experiences, as Tessa did on the day she added apples to her train tracks.

Importantly, all the prekindergarten children write every day—willingly. Brian Kissel was the researcher in this classroom twice a week for two years, and he never heard a child make a fuss about writing.

What This May Mean for Your Classroom

Some of you may be saying, "In my school, we wait to start writing until the second semester of first grade. By that time our kids know their letters and sounds."

If, instead, you start your children out as writers when they are very young, you and your children will find that when they start to write before they know writing represents words, they begin to understand the essence of writing.

Writing is:

- saying something

- putting forth their ideas

- letting other people know what they know

- showing others what they think is important

Words are not the heart of writing; what the young writers have to say is the heart of their writing. Their message is what counts—to them, and to you.

Your very young students, who do not yet know letters, *can* create meaning. They did so as toddlers when they extended their cup toward someone: "Milk!" Little children have things to say and share with others.

The time you set aside for them to be writers, however, is not simply a time for your children to express their thoughts, as they have done for years. It is a time for them to *record* what is important to them. Their thoughts, when they write, are not fleeting. Writing adds permanence, significance to what they have to say.

Your young children need to know that they and their thoughts count. You honor them, and the outward extension of their selves when you celebrate their daily renditions of what they want to tell their friends and you.

Some of you may be saying, "It never occurred to me that drawing is writing."

You have learned to think that writing is words, which, of course, it usually is. You now realize, however, that writing can also be defined as your children's way of telling others what is inside them. It is a hugely complicated, important task, and the sooner you reserve time in your daily schedule for your children to start to learn this crucial process, the more likely they are to internalize its significance.

What you will quickly learn is that some of your children have arrived without writers' hands. They do not know how to use crayons and markers. So, for days they spiral, circle, and explore the somewhat large, plain sheets of paper you will provide. Regardless, you squeeze in beside them every day while they are writing, and you study them with wonder. After a brief moment of appreciation you say something like the following: "It looks like you enjoy writing. What are you writing about?"

Every child writes at a table with other children who are also writing. Intentionally, you have mixed the children at the tables, so those with inexperience are among others who can draw recognizable cars, trees, and people. They hear their new friends talk about their drawings, and they gradually start to create recognizable shapes, such as a school bus, which is a huge, new part of their lives.

As children draw, they talk. You encourage this talk. Young writers, you will soon realize, often talk as they create their representations of a recent class experience or an at-home birthday party. Their words connect their drawings to what they want to say; their words help them realize what they want to say.

Your children's drawings and spoken words will eventually become their drawings and written words.

Some of you may be saying, "I have always had my kids draw and then write."

When your children write across the curriculum, the various curriculum areas present challenges they can meet only by writing, drawing, writing, drawing . . .

This new sequence will be important when your children use writing to figure out new ideas. For young writers, thinking totally in words—or thinking visually and then in words—restrains their explorations and their learning. To use both, whenever one or the other works, helps them to learn as much as possible, and that is what you want!

Closing Thought

Children use drawing as a way to create and convey meaning. When their drawing is respected and valued, children develop complexity in their composition processes over time. To develop as a writer one must try out many strategies and ways to represent a topic.

CHAPTER 2

We Encourage Our Writers to Talk

In order to be writers, many children need to talk among themselves while they write. They ask each other questions about how to make letters, how to spell words, how to draw shapes, and what might happen next in their draft. Sometimes, as a class, they create a piece of writing that may be difficult for the children to compose on their own. At all times, the children's oral language development is extremely important, and encouragement to talk while they write provides them with multiple opportunities as learners.

Snapshot of Five Prekindergarten Writers

We revisit the classroom we just left at the end of the previous chapter, but instead of focusing on Tessa and her apples, we focus on the children's parents' visit to their classroom the previous evening.

The adults rode the same bus to school their children usually ride, and children are excited about what their parents did. They gather on the rug in the corner to tell Miss Robyn what their parents told them and to ask her questions. Then, in her large tablet, Miss Robyn creates her piece of writing for the day. As she engages them in this daily writing demonstration, they continue their conversation with her, focusing on the school bus she has decided to draw.

Then the children walk to their tables, settle in, and we watch and listen as five children at one table write and talk.

Travion begins, "I'm going to draw a car. Not a bus."

Talisha, "Me too. I'm makin' a car today. A police car."

La-Toni moves closer to Talisha, watches her, and asks, "Can you make me a police car?" Talisha focuses in on her police car and doesn't answer right away. La-Toni tries on her own, but doesn't like what she makes. Soon she repeats her request, "I'm trying to make a police car, and I can't make a police car." Talisha says, "Do you know how to draw windows?" drawing one in the air with her finger. La-Toni draws one in her car, and continues to practice windows on the side of her paper:

Talisha's police car

La-Toni's police car and window practice

Meanwhile, Pierson says, "Miss Robyn made a school bus car."

Kallen likes the school bus idea but says, even though he hasn't yet given it a go, "I don't know how to make a school bus. I want Miss Robyn to make me a school bus." With Miss Robyn nowhere nearby, he instead turns to Talisha, "Can you make a yellow school bus for me?" Talisha replies, "I think you can do it. You make it the way *you* think it should be. This is your paper to write on. I'm makin' a police car today." Kallen repeats, "I don't know how to do it!"

Pierson then chimes in, "I made a school bus!"

Talisha nods to Kallen, "Ask Pierson how he did his. Don't ask him to do it for you. Just ask him to show you." So Pierson gives Kallen a bit of instruction, thinking as he talks. "I make the big this," he says pointing to the largest shape in his drawing, "and then I did this," he says, pointing to the shape within the large shape. Then he appears to have figured out what he did, and clarifies, "I made a circle. Then I made another circle."

Pierson's bus

Kallen, who still doesn't try, says, "I still don't know how to do it." Talisha repeats her earlier advice, "Well, why don't you do it the way you think you are supposed to do it. I'm making a police. I want to be a police when I grow up." Kallen starts to work, and after several minutes, says, "I just made a person instead. I made a person instead because I can't make a bus. I'm making a grandpa and a boy. That's what I'm going to do instead."

Kallen's grandpa and a boy

Interspersed within the above conversation have been comments by Travion, the boy who started the conversation about cars. At one time, he repeats, "I'm making myself a car." After a few minutes, however, he pauses, studies it, looks around at Pierson's bus and Talisha's police car, looks at his own paper again, sees a curve he likes, and says, "I'm makin' me a blue rainbow." Soon, finished with his blue rainbow, and seeing La-Toni practice squares, Travion says, "I'm makin' a house. I'm makin' a building."

Tavions's car, blue rainbow, house, and building

What These Writers Can Do: Strengths and Breakthroughs

- Talisha pays close attention to words she hears during her teacher's demonstration; she uses her teacher's language to break down tasks her friends want to learn how to do. And she doesn't let them off the hook—they have to give it a go in their *own* way!

- La-Toni repeatedly requests help from the other young writers at her table. She knows she can count on them for support when she tries something different, and she takes Talisha's demonstration seriously. La-Toni practices making windows.

- Pierson can explain his drawing process—of his bus—to his classmate. He breaks his process down into a sequence and describes his shapes in terms of their approximate size.

- Tavion understands the nature of an evolving draft, from a car to a blue rainbow to a house to a building! He samples bits and pieces from the drafts he sees around him, trying them on his paper. This is what authors do—use other writing as a springboard for their own. Who knows what will evolve?

- Kallen chooses to draw figures that are familiar to him, but he knows there are new shapes and concepts to try. He has seen Miss Robyn's writing and the writing of his peers, and he stores their ideas for another day.

Snapshot of Co-Authors

A Second-Grade Class

We now move into second grade and find the young writers engaged in a unit of study about the history of their city: Richmond, Virginia. Previous to their study, teacher Tena Freeman searched for children's books about Richmond's history and found none, so the class decided to write and publish one. As preparation, they took a walking tour of the historic area near their school and field trips to various notable city sites. Plus, they studied their city via other sources of information, including guidebooks, pamphlets, maps, and so on.

On days previous to our snapshot the students began composing their book, and this is its first page—as it later appeared in published form:

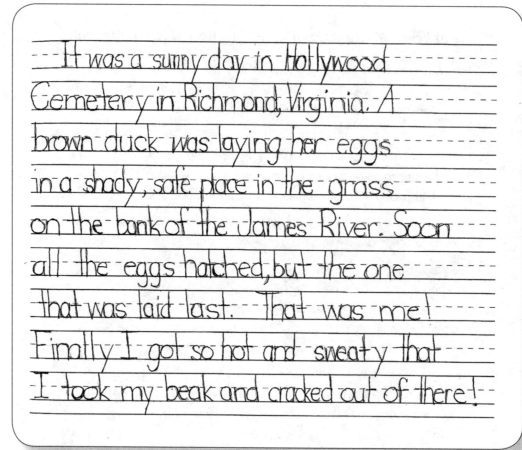

It was a sunny day in Hollywood Cemetery in Richmond, Virginia. A brown duck was laying her eggs in a shady, safe place in the grass on the bank of the James River. Soon all the eggs hatched, but the one that was laid last. That was me! Finally I got so hot and sweaty that I took my beak and cracked out of there!

As the children's story evolves, this new duckling finds himself alone in the world and searches for his mother throughout historic Richmond. His escapades are sometimes far-fetched as the children want their book to be funny—this is second grade, after all! In addition, the children choose to start right out with history; the duckling is born in Hollywood Cemetery, located close to their school, where several former U.S. presidents are buried.

Today, the class moves the story forward, and Mrs. Freeman picks up on where their conversation ended yesterday with Janine's suggestion, "How about we let the duckling come to St. Andrew's School to meet us? But how can he get from the cemetery to our school?"

Aimarra thinks aloud, "I live near the cemetery and I've heard the cannons being shot on special occasions."

Lily can hardly contain herself as she suggests, "What if the duckling crawls into the cannon to sleep. Then—oh, it will have to be a holiday—a man fires up the cannon and accidentally shoots the duckling to our school, a half a block away!"

"Brilliant, Lily!" smiles Mrs. Freeman, as several classmates give Lily a thumbs-up.

Cory picks right up on Lily's suggestion, and adds, "How about he lands in our basketball net?"

"He'd fall through," someone worries.

"Cory's idea is great, though. He is on to something," confirms Mrs. Freeman. "What else is soft on our school grounds?"

They resolve their concern, the conversation continues, and Mrs. Freeman records their ideas on a chart. After several weeks of working on their masterpiece a few minutes every day, it is finished. Everyone prints or illustrates a part of it, and Mrs. Freeman sends it off to the publisher, Nationwide Learning, Inc. Each child receives a hardcover copy, and so does their school library!

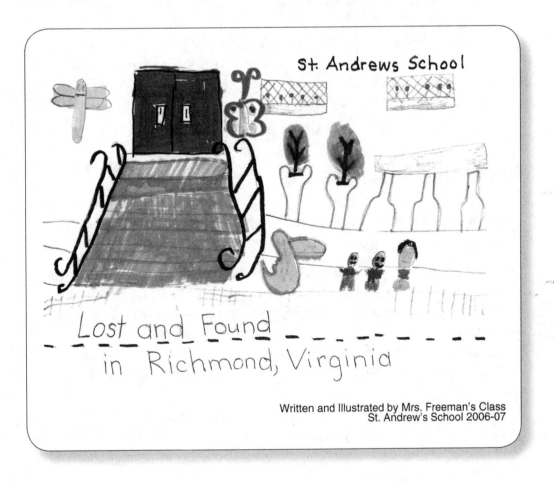

St. Andrews School

Lost and Found in Richmond, Virginia

Written and Illustrated by Mrs. Freeman's Class
St. Andrew's School 2006-07

What These Writers Can Do: Strengths and Breakthroughs

These writers learn about historical fiction by writing the first-ever historical fiction book for children about their city! They gain their information from multiple sources and study the genre of historical fiction by reading and studying children's literature. They start a years-long trek of being able to read from the inside out. As writers, they learn how historical fiction is supposed to work.

These second graders problem solve as they think of where to start the story, who will be the main characters, and how they will write themselves into the story. Each day, as they begin, they reread what they wrote the previous day and ask questions to determine what should come next, a vital task for writers engaged in the creation of a long text. They create ongoing text that satisfies their readers' predictions of what will happen next—a hugely important task of writers. Overall, these young writers develop an awareness that the pieces of the story must tie together sensibly.

They realize that every student has something important to offer to the story. This appreciation for all brings their class together, strengthens their efforts as writers, and lends to their ability to create a community—a concept we will revisit when we rejoin this class in Chapter 3.

What the Teachers Do

The prekindergarten teacher places high value on her children's emerging oral language.

Miss Robyn moves among her writers as they work; often, she remains quiet, listening and observing. She wants the children to talk among themselves, not to become dependent on her. As writers they must depend on themselves and each other.

As she observes, Miss Robyn listens to their language. Many of them are *makin'* something, so she tells herself to be careful to always use the words *drawing* or *writing*.

She hears the words of the confident children, such as Talisha, who drew a police car, and Pierson, who drew a bus. And Miss Robyn notices the children who are hesitant, such as Kallen, who couldn't bring himself to try a car or bus, but who knows he can draw grandpa and a boy.

She hears the words of the children who try new ideas, such as La-Toni's windows and Travion's car, blue rainbow, house, and building. By being present, Miss Robyn not only sees what her children create, she hears what they say as they work; this is how she comes to know them as writers.

On this exact day a researcher (Brian Kissel, a colleague of ours) studied these five children intensely and recorded their talk; on her own, Ms. Robyn cannot do this, but she is always among her children as they write, in order to hear, see, and learn as much as possible about their writing processes—so she knows what to teach.

Given what she notices, Miss Robyn considers the following:

- She is careful to use precise language when she reads children's literature to the children; she refers to the title, author, and uses other book language.

- Miss Robyn chooses her words carefully when she engages the children in her daily demonstrations; at the beginning of the year when our snapshot occurred and writing was in the form of drawing for her children, she used the terms *square*, *triangle*, and *circle* for elements of her drawings/writing.

- When her young writers ask her for help she defers. Instead, she teaches them how to request help from their tablemates. Before long, children do not come to her for assistance, unless she is sitting at their table and already interacting with them.

The teacher of the second-grade class engages them in conversations about what each sentence sets up their readers to want to know, so, as writers, they can supply the answers to their readers' predictions.

Mrs. Freeman and her second-grade children decide to take on a task that no one else has ever tried—to write a historical fiction picture book about their city, Richmond. Knowing this to be a difficult task, they decide to co-author it.

Also, worried that this lengthy task could tire the children, Mrs. Freeman decides to engage her co-authors only for a few minutes every day instead of expecting them to participate in lengthy sessions.

Daily, they gather to reread what they have written, remind themselves of their plans, and create a new section of text. As they offer ideas, suggest counter ideas, and build upon each other's contributions, their talk leads their story carefully forward.

The conversations, importantly, served another function. During other parts of the day while they composed as single authors, the words they uttered as co-authors sometimes resounded, reminding them to keep their overall plan in mind and to look closely at how each sentence leads into the next.

The children in Mrs. Freeman's second grade learned some important lessons. When they met to co-author their picture book, they offered suggestions, weighed options, and their talk led their historical fiction forward.

Overall, Mrs. Freeman gave her class this opportunity to co-author because she could use this occasion to:

- demonstrate how writing works.

- show that every child has something to contribute to the writing of a story.

- teach her students how they can learn from one another.

- reveal how individual ideas, when combined, can be better than only one person's idea.

- help the children feel the reward of completing a task as a team.

- teach that a large task can be finished by breaking it into small segments.

Writer-Friendly Classroom Features

The Prekindergarten Classroom

If you had listened in as these children wrote on this day, you would not have heard the clear talk as we presented it in the snapshot. Often, a conversation started, another entered, the original resumed, a third conversation began, and the original reentered. More than one line of thinking was always in play.

Also, you would have realized that these children are learning to work together. Even though it is still early in the year you may, however, have worried about Kallen. Or not. He does say, correctly, that he can make grandpa and a boy. At the same time, no one gives him the help he requested so he can make a bus.

Miss Robyn teaches the children what to say and how to help—a difficult task for four-year-olds engaged in writing. They, do, of course, become much better.

Importantly, these young writers know they *can* talk. These writers know that no one expects them to write in silence. They *must* talk in order to move forward as writers!

Also, these children want to learn how to do new things. They regularly request help, try new ideas, and refine their fine-motor skills. Along the way, Miss Robyn shows them how to make various shapes, objects—and letters. She tries to stay just one small baby-step ahead of them, nudging them into new territory.

Importantly, the children intentionally move forward as writers. In this writer-friendly classroom they do not have to worry about receiving negative response from Miss Robyn. She never (yes, never) provides a young writer with a negative response. They write without fear of placing incorrect marks on their papers.

They do evaluate themselves, as we saw and heard. They set their own standards and work to accomplish greater and more difficult tasks.

Independence from Miss Robyn is a key goal of hers as soon as the school year begins. She does not make marks on their papers! This writer-friendly feature is one she (and all of us!) learned from Quandra, as you read in the Introduction to this book.

These young writers' writing is important—and everyone honors it. The children know: *We* are writers.

The Second-Grade Classroom

If you had visited the second-grade classroom while the children composed their historical fiction, you would have seen them clustered around Mrs. Freeman, heard their contributions, heard her encouragement, and seen her write their words on a chart.

This daily engagement kept their study of history alive for an extended period of time. Their words kept their thoughts alive, and they learned about the possibility of writing a text over many weeks. Importantly, they heard the value of others' contributions and how their story benefitted from the words of many.

Before long, however, you would find yourself immersed in the mystery of their duckling's experiences. The children's excitement is contagious as they listen to each other's words, lean forward, can't wait to offer their contributions, and learn to build their comments on preceding thoughts.

What This May Mean for Your Classroom

Some of you may be saying, "When the children in my classroom talk they often talk about something totally unrelated to what they are writing."

Yes, that is common, and it is just fine—for a while. In fact, at the university level when the teachers in our classes meet in small groups to discuss their writing, they often diverge. That is just what talk does—it wanders.

Importantly, the seemingly off-task talk often leads back to the writing. When you listen patiently to your young writers, you will often hear them acquire details for the writing they are working on at the moment, as well as ideas for future writing.

At the same time, some writers who are engaged in their work may not appreciate lots of talk at the table where they are working, so you may want to provide a place in the classroom where they can go, on their own, to write quietly.

Some of you who teach second grade may want to create a five-minute period of silence at some point during writing time, making sure that the children may talk as they write the rest of the time.

If you do find that some children appear to talk excessively, you will want to carefully observe their productivity as writers. If they seem to be unengaged as writers, their problem is not talk. The problem is lack of engagement in their writing, and you will bend over backward to help those writers find something to write about that compels their hearts and pencils.

Some of you may be saying, "When I hold an all-class session only a few students participate, and it tends to be the same ones every time."

This is a common concern. In general, you probably have two types of students who don't participate in your whole-class discussions.

Some have many great ideas but they are basically shy and/or not assertive. They seldom manage to work their way into the large conversation. You, as the teacher, will be the assertive one in this case. You may keep two charts going—one for the ongoing story the class is writing and one for the comments children offer. On the latter you may provide the name of the child who contributed each comment, and you strive to include all names before someone can provide a second thought.

Some children still may not contribute, and you may want to privately confer with those children to find out why. Maybe a child is not engaged for acceptable reasons; maybe she is thinking, wondering—and totally comfortable with not entering the conversation. Maybe, however, the child is not interested. Maybe that child needs to be the one up front who records the names of the children who offer suggestions for the story. Maybe that child, when you confer with her, will provide you with an insight that will alter your instruction so she will become engaged.

Importantly, for children who are unengaged in a class story, you—and the class—will work together to bring everyone into the act.

You will read more about this same class—and how they learn to work together—in the next chapter.

Closing Thought

In the prekindergarten and second-grade classrooms profiled in this chapter, the teachers create an environment that encourages talk. The children work in close proximity. The physical arrangement of the prekindergarten writers at tables and the second graders in a cluster invites interactions. Talk among children is important, and talk among young writers is very important. Rather than honor the age-old fear that children who talk will get out of hand, we promote talk that enables them as learners of content and helps them learn about writers and writing. Their oral language and written language develop in tandem. To use both is paramount.

CHAPTER 3

We Create Communities of Interested Classmates

Writers can't hide; their words are out there for others to read. This can frighten young children who may not possess a lot of confidence. They need to know that others want to know them, want to listen to their writing, and want to come to know them as individuals with interesting ideas and experiences to share. For children new to our country, writing can be daunting. But when they work amid an inviting class of writers who obviously enjoy each other's drafts, newcomers and English language learners want to become writers, too. Similarly, children whose personal concerns lead them to see themselves as outsiders can become writers when they appreciate their classmates' intentional efforts to bring them into their class circle of friends.

Snapshot of Jamil

A Kindergarten Writer

We now turn to kindergarten and focus on Jamil, a refugee child from Africa who has recently arrived in this country. His English is sparse, and his teacher, Sue Harris, works hard to make him feel welcome. One day, in a special effort to show her interest, Mrs. Harris showed the children a map of Africa to explain where

Jamil had come from. When Jamil heard the word "Africa," he put his head in his lap, covered his head, and shouted, "No! No!"

During their daily writing workshop, Jamil draws objects, names them in English as he tells others what they are, and volunteers to share his work during their all-class share. Sometimes during their writing workshop his serious face breaks into a smile—he appears to enjoy being among his classmates while they write. Jamil closely watches the children at his table as they spontaneously read their writing to each other, but he does not participate in these child-to-child conversations. Still, it seems he very much wants to become more of a central part of this busy classroom. And he does not want to be reminded that he's from another place. Jamil, however, has yet to learn the language and the ways of his classroom that will ease his entry. Then, happily, Jamil figures out on his own that writing can help him in this endeavor!

One day, when Jenesse Evertson, the researcher in his kindergarten, walks into the classroom, she sees a crowd of children around Jamil. It is mid-November and Jamil is drawing the children in the class wearing these rectangular-shaped hats:

Jamil's "Name Hats"

Looking up at Mrs. Evertson he says with a smile, "Name Hats." Jamil is *the* center of attention. He has found his way in! Jamil has figured out how to couple his drawings with words to bring himself into this community of interested writers.

Mrs. Evertson wonders where he got the idea for these hats and she manages to ask him in a way he understands. Quickly, Jamil opens a picture dictionary to a drawing of a cowboy hat, and says, "Cowboy." This, apparently, was the genesis of his "Name Hats." He then used the children's name cards, visible in various places around the room, to learn how to copy their names onto hats.

His idea excites the other children—they all want a "Name Hat," and this writing thrives for days.

Jamil's process of creating the Name Hats helps him establish his place as an effective writer and communicator in his classroom community. His peers now begin to seek out Jamil's guidance in drawing people, a skill many of them admire, and this young boy gathers confidence as others want to emulate him. Importantly, his Name Hats become Jamil's signature contribution. Throughout the year, a Name Hat appears when Jamil wants to offer a gesture of friendship to another child, and many figures in drawings that accompany his pieces of writing wear Name Hats.

What This Writer Can Do: Strengths and Breakthroughs

- Jamil recognizes the power in a name. Just as we learned from Quandra in the introduction to this book, a name written on paper is more than just a string of letters. Jamil understands that, and introduces himself to his community of writers by coupling their names with his drawings.

- Jamil is an astute observer. Closely watching his peers' spontaneous, excited responses to one another's writings gives him insight into how he can use writing to establish relationships. Importantly, Jamil figures out how to become a member of his classroom community of writers!

- Jamil develops a "signature" for himself as a writer. His Name Hats become a way of putting his individual marker on his drafts. In the parlance of the world of writing, he is developing his own unique writer's voice.

Snapshot of Leroy

A Second-Grade Writer

We now return to the same second-grade classroom in which the children wrote the historical fiction picture book. At this particular time, however, teacher Tena

Freeman is worried. Leroy, a new child in the class, has become increasingly in need of attention and seeks it in negative ways. Mrs. Freeman has tried to remain supportive and always insists that the other children treat him with respect, but his adjustment is not going well, and she is wondering what to do.

Twice a week, Mrs. Freeman leads the class in a Friendship Circle experience, and today is one of those days. As usual, she draws a circle on the board and says, "If you feel that you are getting along with your classmates, write your name *in* the circle, if you are just so-so with your friends, write your name *on* the circle, and if you feel that you're having trouble making friends, please write your name *outside* the circle."

Leroy writes his name outside. He is not the only child who feels outside; another child placed his name there before it was Leroy's turn but, at this time, the children listen to Leroy. He talks, the children talk, and they start to think of what they all can do, say, and write so Leroy will not feel that he is "outside their classroom circle." Gradually, via this experience and others, the youngsters become more sensitive to Leroy's feelings.

In a few weeks, it is spring break, and when they return, the tide seems to have turned, as Leroy writes this note and reads it to the class. In it we hear, among other things, that he has missed Mrs. Freeman's stories about her grandchildren:

Good morning class
On Spring break I just was
missing all of you because I
don't have anyone to be funny
or tell good story a dout gran-
children I don't have someone
to go out of there mind it is
like on cowbells when the father
was going on trips, and he said
I was Just missing his two
twens.

"Good morning class, On spring break I just was missing all of you because I don't have anyone to be funny [with] or tell good stories about grandchildren. I don't have someone to go out of their mind. It is like on Cowbells where the father was going on trips and he said, 'I was just missing his [my] two twins.'"

What This Writer Can Do: Strengths and Breakthroughs

- Leroy realizes that his classroom community is a safe place in which to be truthful about his feelings of being on the outside. He sees how others take risks in expressing themselves during the Friendship Circle and then takes his own, first by writing that one important word: his name.

- Leroy accepts his classmates' explanations of what has been happening. They are used to playing with children who have been at the school in kindergarten and first grade, but Leroy is new. Once they understand how Leroy feels, the students respond with support for him in the classroom and his need for playmates when they are outside.

- Leroy uses writing to express himself. He experiments with written words to tell his classmates about his spring break, and he does so in a letter format. He has something important to say and steps forward to read aloud to the class—from his newly created position inside the circle.

What the Teachers Do

Jamil's kindergarten teacher provides time for her children to write about whatever they want, in whatever form they want, four days each week.

Mrs. Harris provides the children with open-ended writing opportunities in order to foster their success as writers and to give them opportunities to claim writing as a resource they personally own and enjoy. As a result, a classroom community evolves in which each child can figure out a way to become recognized as a writer—a person with *author*-ity.

If Mrs. Harris had always told Jamil what to write about, and how to write it, her topics and forms may not have appealed to him. Or, if she only gave the children occasional opportunities to make these decisions, some of the children may not have found a way to create a place for themselves in their community of writers. Specifically, Jamil may not have found a way to use writing as his breakthrough into English and as his way to earn a place in his classroom community where his classmates respect him for both his writing and drawing ability.

Mrs. Harris creates a classroom in which her kindergarten writers know when it is time to write. They understand that their teacher expects them to think of something to say and a way to say it that will interest both her and the other students.

Discovering their voices as writers—with something important to say and the ability to express it—is both intellectually invigorating and a tremendous confidence builder.

In order to strengthen her children's sense of self, Mrs. Harris intentionally creates a community of writers and learners as she:

- teaches her children to interact with her while she writes during her demonstration lessons.

- teaches them how to read/share their writing with their class for response.

- teaches her students how to respond to each other with interest.

Leroy's second-grade teacher strives to create a Community of Interested Writers who support each other throughout the day.

Mrs. Freeman knows that the Reading and Writing Workshop in her classroom will be as strong as possible if their Community of Interested Writers is in place throughout the day; indeed, Mrs. Freeman and her children meet regularly to discuss the importance of their words, actions, and feelings. When Leroy did not think his classmates liked him, this thought overwhelmed him at recess, during math—and during writing.

Writing is difficult, and young writers are sensitive. They will step out and try new strategies when they know beyond a doubt that their attempts will be met with appreciation and encouragement. This necessary environment that encourages reflection thrives when the teacher encourages risk-taking and experimentation throughout the day.

The children in Mrs. Freeman's second-grade class know that when they enter their classroom door, they enter a Community of Interested Writers who write, listen, and support one another. They do this because their teacher:

- encourages a community spirit of learning during occasions when the entire class authors pieces of writing, as they did when they wrote about historical Richmond. As Mrs. Freeman records the students' messages and ideas, the children see how writing works. They produce compositions together that are better than what many of them could have written individually. And this process of fitting their various ideas together lends itself to a willingness to share concerns.

- values the children's words.

- shares bits of her own life with the students, as we learned when Leroy referred to Mrs. Freeman's stories about her grandchildren. Sharing important pieces of her life encourages the children to do likewise, becoming better acquainted with each other.

Writer-Friendly Classroom Features

Jamil's Kindergarten Classroom

As you enter Jamil's classroom and look for him—on the day of our snapshot—you see him in the midst of a cluster of children. This is the middle of their writing workshop, and they are gathering around him to receive the gifts he is offering them—his drawings of them wearing their Name Hats.

This was a turning point of Jamil's year, a landmark day. For many days he had sat silently amid his classmates while they spontaneously talked about their writing as they wrote, his limited English keeping him from participating in these conversations. And, even though the children had responded with interest to his drawings when he shared with the class, he still felt disconnected.

On this special day, however, Jamil experienced a breakthrough, and you could feel the electricity in the room.

This scene became possible, in part, because Mrs. Harris uses name cards to introduce children to print and to each other. The children can find their names at various places around the room such as the name attendance board, on their cubbies, and on the coat rack, marking each child's coat hook—and they refer to them often.

Often, children's written names become their entries into written language. Through their continuous study of written names—their own, classmates', and their favorite characters in books—they learn about similarities in the printed form of names and the importance of capital letters for these special identity labels.

In addition, Mrs. Harris designates a space for each child at a table and marks it with the child's name card. While the children are free to move about the room while they write—in order to share with and learn from each other—

they have a space at a table to call their own. This is very important to these children; many come from crowded homes with essentially no space to call their own.

Overall, the kindergarten children's writing varies tremendously, which Jamil has seen, so to create his classmates' likenesses with Name Hats is entirely appropriate. He is learning to create writing that is important to him, that serves his needs and purposes. Jamil becomes a writer who knows how to use writing to garner the interest of his classmates, win social acceptance, and to achieve a breakthrough in his English learning.

Leroy's Second-Grade Classroom

Although this class seemed very connected and supportive of one another in the previous snapshot of their creation of a class book, new classmates sometimes test the community. Entering the class on the day of the Friendship Circle and witnessing Leroy's actions, you may feel a bit uncomfortable or amazed.

At the least, you may find this scene unusual. At the research team meeting when Dorothy Suskind first wrote about Leroy placing himself outside the circle, most of us had never—in our many collective years of experience—been privy to such a scene.

It showed us that our writing workshops, or reading and writing workshops, will not thrive as peaceful islands amid turmoil. The classroom community of writers and learners must work supportively throughout the day.

The Friendship Circle, on this day, was a turning point for Leroy. A feeling of relief went around the circle when students responded to Leroy's concerns with encouraging words. He could become one of them now.

Leroy was better able to enjoy writing when he arrived each day. He became more confident as a writer as he learned new skills in the mini-lessons, conferred with Mrs. Freeman during the reading/writing workshop, and shared his writing with supportive classmates.

In this snapshot about Leroy's transformation, one must realize that writing across the curriculum isn't just writing about math and other curriculum areas. It is writing about math and other curriculum areas *in the midst of a classroom community* in which the children intentionally work to build their supportive bonds of friendship and caring throughout the day. It is profoundly significant that Leroy eventually felt comfortable enough to express his feelings—and had at his disposal the power of writing.

What This May Mean for Your Classroom

Some of you, as you read about Jamil's Name Hats, may have been thinking, "I don't let my children write about the same thing every day."

We have all had that young writer who writes excessively about the same topic. "Another story about dinosaurs!" you say to yourself as you scratch your head in exhaustion. But this repetition, as it turns out, often plays a hugely important role.

Often, when your writers delve continuously into a topic, they are actually engaged in an exercise of "coming to know." They need and/or want this practice time. The act of continuously reconstructing a topic can bring your young writers into the comfort levels they need. It is in this safe place, in the middle of composition, that they can break out and take chances—and eventually try on new hats—in which they can experiment with how to connect themselves to the other writers in your classroom.

These repetitions can also serve as "shout-outs" to the other children and to you. They say, "I am trying to find out where I belong. I am not sure how to relate to you and my classmates, but I would sure like to join this classroom." Eventually, as each of your children studies your classroom, watches the other writers, interacts with you and the other children when you read children's literature, and interacts during your writing demonstrations, each child becomes comfortable. In a few cases, this may take months, as you will see in Chapter 8.

Importantly, watch for slight changes when a child seemingly engages in repetition for a long period of time. Sometimes you will actually see slight changes in drawings or a story line. These new features may show growth, and you will want to learn about them when you confer with this writer. As you saw in Chapter 1, a very young writer wrote train tracks for days—and then she changed—a change brought on by interest in the school curriculum.

Overall, your young writers, like more experienced writers, will sometimes build a name for themselves in the classroom or in the publishing world by becoming comfortable with and engaging in a continuous exploration of one topic. So, instead of scratching your head and sighing the next time Mary starts another dinosaur story, you may want to think to yourself, "What does this dinosaur have that yesterday's dinosaur did not?" Or, "What is Mary trying to teach herself, her classmates, and me about who she is and what she needs?"

Some of you may be saying, "Our school is under heavy pressure to meet state standards, as measured by standardized assessments. I don't have time for the social curriculum."

We arrive at school each day with a flurry of goals tapping us on the shoulder and they shout in unison, "Hurry up! You have so much to accomplish today!" You see one child bully another in the hallway, and you think, "We have to get to our grammar lesson. I simply do not have time for this nonsense." But you pause. You know that your children are more willing to grow and take risks in their learning when you pause. The young writers under your wing must know you love them, personally care about them, and intentionally create a community in which they feel the support of all.

Sometimes, however, when you become overwhelmed, you may put more emphasis on the test than the child. He, then, will put his emphasis on the one thing he feels you are not attending to—how can he fit in and what roles should he play inside the four walls of the classroom? Today, your one student may have had those worries at the back of his mind when he bullied the other.

Children, like us, are social beings. They learn as they talk with the writers in your classroom, push each other on the swing set, and play with each other during recess. And if a child's conversational words are met with silence or rebuked, she assumes she simply does not matter and the conversation and the learning and the growth simply stop. This stalemate cripples the child and is going to do nothing for your school's test scores.

After all, the content in social studies, science, mathematics, and reading mean nothing if Mary has emotionally separated herself from you and her fellow learners. A child who is emotionally and socially engaged in the classroom culture is a child who will push herself to work beyond her comfort zone and in turn will learn the content you want to teach. She can become a writer.

So, the social curriculum is not an add-on or a burden; it is the prerequisite for all learning that will transpire in your classroom today.

Some of you may be saying, "I don't feel comfortable sharing my personal life with my students."

We are teachers. What does that mean? Is it a job or a calling or perhaps a way of being in the world? At its best, it calls us to challenge our boys and girls to take chances with their learning and step on to new terrain—not knowing if they have what it takes. They take chances.

Your students trust you enough to tell you who they are, where they live, and what is happening in their hearts and homes. This willingness to be raw and open grows great learners and great citizens. But it is rare that a young child will walk out on that limb if she does not view herself in a close give-and-take relationship with you, her teacher. She wants to know that you love to ride horses, ride a bicycle, and bake brownies. This information is not trivial or trivia, it is part of our being. It is what brings students together as best friends and creates favorite teachers. It leads your students to picture what you are doing outside the gates of school.

As your children write their lives across the curriculum, you will share your life within your writing lessons or bring in your uncle the firefighter during the unit on Community Helpers. Your self makes your writing yours as your children's selves make their writing uniquely theirs. The children in your classroom are willing to write their lives across the day in large part because you show them how as you do likewise.

Closing Thought

Writers grow when they are surrounded by others who show interest in them *and* their work. Given flexibility to find a writing idea, genre, and format that works for them and appeals to their classmates, children become writers. This is especially true when a classroom rests on the philosophy that the circle of writers and learners intentionally includes everyone throughout the day—no one should ever be "outside the circle." It takes a village to raise a writer.

At the same time, young writers want to be citizens of the village. They intentionally find their way into this new space—this community of writers—through their drawings, talk, and interactions. It is, however, not only difficult to become a full-fledged writer within the circle—writing itself is difficult!

Again, our children persist. As they navigate their way through this new territory, they start to pay closer attention to the conventions that help them say what they want to say. In the first three chapters we heard and saw their words as they experimented with new texts in various ways. We now turn our attention to what these young writers do with what they have put onto paper. We begin by shrinking the more conceptual notions of space into those more tangible spaces—the ones that literally separate words on the page.

CHAPTER 4

We Encourage Our Writers to Experiment with Spaces

In the first section of this book, we looked closely at what young writers do as they figure out how to create a meaningful message on paper—they were learning the essence of what it means to become a writer. Drawing, talk, and their classmates helped them see the importance of developing a voice on paper.

So what happens next? In the next three chapters we show how young writers can clarify their messages. To do this, they make their writing look like the print they see around them and in their favorite children's literature. The more they write, the more they connect the print they create with the print they see on other pages.

This is a tricky leap for them, as young writers aren't always sure where words end and begin. When they talk they don't leave spaces between words, so when they write, their words touch. The children soon learn, however, that they can't read these chains of letters, so they create strategies to help them read their work.

Their evolution as writers and readers goes hand in hand; each one enables and informs the other.

Snapshot of Emily

A Kindergarten Writer

Five kindergarten children write at a table. One of them is Emily. For three days, Emily has been writing about the wild ponies of Chincoteague, a famous vacation spot in Virginia that she will soon visit with her family. Today, Emily draws two horses, Sea Star and Misty, based on the classic children's literature book by Marguerite Henry, *Misty of Chincoteague* (1947/1975). As Emily draws, she talks to anyone at her table who may be listening, "My mom read me the book about Misty and Sea Star," and Jenesse Evertson, the researcher at the table, records Emily's words.

As her illustration spans onto the adjacent page in her journal, Emily continues to narrate her writing process, "This is a looooong story."

Mrs. Evertson asks Emily a question about the horses and they talk about them as Emily draws. Next, Emily begins to place words under her illustration. When she has written four letters and drawn a vertical line, she says, "Sea Star," and points to the vertical line after the R. "A finger," she says. Earlier that day, in her mini-lesson, Mrs. Evertson had placed a real finger between her words, and now Emily has decided to use lines to represent fingers—to represent spaces. Emily finishes her writing with two more "fingers," and reads it aloud to Mrs. Evertson and anyone else at her table that wants to listen, "Sea Star and Misty were playing together."

"Sea Star and Misty were playing together."

Importantly, as she reads her final three words, she hesitates and rereads. Without "fingers" to separate them, that part of her text was a bit harder to read.

What This Writer Can Do: Strengths and Breakthroughs

- Emily develops a strategy that allows her to clarify her thoughts as she writes: drawing a line. Because it is difficult for young writers to hear the breaks between words in speech or thought, to do so on paper by inserting finger spaces is not only unnatural but laborious, as well. To write with one hand and physically sound out the message—all the while trying to keep the paper steady—and add the additional hand movement needed to insert a finger space . . . goodness! That's a lot for a young writer! Clever Emily finds a solution to this problem. Importantly, she sets off names in her draft. For many young writers, the name is an important starting point, as we learned from both Quandra in our Introduction and Jamil in Chapter 3. So, when Emily experiments with spaces, it is not surprising that the first words she sets off are the names of the characters in her piece of writing.

- Emily writes about a piece of children's literature. Not only does her mother read to her, Mrs. Harris, her kindergarten teacher, reads to the class *twice* each day. Some of the children in this classroom had not heard someone read to them until they stepped through her classroom door on the first day of school, so Mrs. Harris must immerse them in books, in words, in print, in the world of writers.

- Emily rereads her writing to check for meaning. To learn to reread is very important, and we create this habit. The children reread their writing all the time— just as Mrs. Harris rereads books to them. They read all kinds of print, over and over again.

Snapshot of Frederick
Another Kindergarten Writer

Frederick sits at the same table as Emily. A few days later he, too, begins to experiment with spaces. A young NASCAR fan, Frederick creates a draft about a race, drawing three cars racing for the flag, and a talking bubble coming out of the winner's mouth, "Yea" (JBH).

"Done," he announces to no one in particular.

"You're faster than those cars!" says Mrs. Evertson, who is sitting at his table on this day. She engages him in a conversation about a recent NASCAR race, and then encourages his growth as a writer by saying, "Let's see if you can add some more words to your picture."

"Okay," says Frederick as he barely pauses to think. "I'll write *race car*."

Orally, he stretches out the word *rrraccce*, and Emily, the girl who wrote about Sea Star and Misty on an earlier day, helps him locate *R* and *S* on the alphabet strip at their table. After Frederick writes the word, he puts his pencil under it and reads it speedily, "*Race*. I have to say it fast, like the *race*." He reads it quickly again, with emphasis, "*Race!*"

"Now, *car*," he says, as he places his whole hand on the paper next to *race*. "A space," he says.

"You just need a finger," reminds Emily, already the expert!

"No. Listen to how you say it." Frederick says, "*Race*" rapidly, hesitates for a dramatic pause, and then says, "*Car*. It's more than a finger. It's a hand." Frederick lifts his hand from his paper and writes *KR*. Unfortunately, when he lifts his hand, he loses his space!

Racecar
"Yea!"

Quick to recover, and undaunted by the missing space, Frederick says, "Oh, well! I'll just say it like this, *Racecar!*" And he does.

What This Writer Can Do: Strengths and Breakthroughs

- Frederick knows how to separate *race car* into two words and intends to do so. He creates, with his hand, the space he needs to divide it into two parts. This is his first time doing this, however, and only a few seconds later, when he actually writes, his pencil forgets to leave the space his hand created! Undaunted, Frederick adjusts to his text. Instead of reading, "Race Car," he reads, "Racecar." This young reader/writer thinks deeply about the importance of each word—and space—in a piece of writing.

- Frederick sounds out his *r* and his *s* to get the letters onto the page, practices saying "Race Car" before he writes it, and reads it again after he writes it. He reads aloud to hear how his writing sounds—just as professional writers do in their heads. He experiments—trying to hear the significance of a possible space. For many adults, writing is an interior activity; we read our writing in our heads as we compose, and *then* we read it aloud. For young children, however, writing is both a mental and physical experience.

- Frederick knows that, depending upon its function, text can be written in different places on the page. He writes a word in a talking bubble at the source of the action and writes another at the top of his paper to serve as a title.

What the Teacher Does

Emily and Frederick's kindergarten teacher demonstrates new strategies but does not require her writers to use them right away.

Every day, Sue Harris—or another adult—creates her own daily piece of writing as the children sit in a cluster around her. As she writes, she talks, and the children interact with her. On the day Emily experimented with spaces, Jenesse Evertson had created a piece of writing for this demonstration, and she had placed her finger between her words as she composed, talked, and responded to the children's spontaneous comments. For some time, the adults in this classroom had written with words during their mini-lessons, and silently—without fingers—placed spaces between words. Today, however, the spaces were the aim of the lesson. Mrs. Evertson pointed out to the children what she was doing. A few children had started to use spaces, so it appeared to be time to point out to the class the intentional way writers insert spaces of non-text into their strings of text.

When she finished her writing, Mrs. Evertson invited the children to try creating spaces when they wrote that day. The timeline of when children develop a concept of word varies tremendously, so Mrs. Evertson did not tell them they must create spaces between words. She knows if she were to say that, she may cause anxiety within some of them.

On a subsequent day, when conferring with Frederick while he wrote, Mrs. Evertson encouraged him to write more, and when he did, she learned that he does know about spaces between words (and a lot about words, in general!), even though she had not seen evidence of this in his writing. From now on, in order to help him build on his understanding of the concept of word, the adults in the classroom will encourage him to write more than one word and to either leave spaces between them or place them in distinct places within his draft, such as within speech bubbles.

And don't forget Emily. She just may insist that Frederick remember spaces! In addition, Mrs. Harris:

- sometimes uses her finger to highlight words when she reads big books and other children's literature.

- points out how authors use spaces for special effects in big books and other children's literature.

- encourages the children to notice spaces between words in their daily environment.

By pointing out spaces in these various contexts, Mrs. Harris invites children to look closely at how print appears on paper. When it comes time for them to experiment on their own, they gradually begin to develop strategies to make their own writing convey more clearly the messages they have in mind.

Writer-Friendly Classroom Features

Every day, these kindergarten children write with the adults in the room conferring with them as they write. The adults provide this attention in order to foster the young writers' success.

Importantly, the children know their teachers are primarily interested in *what* they are writing about. Mrs. Evertson engaged Frederick in a conversation about a NASCAR race, and Emily in a conversation about the small horses.

Then the children's new efforts in the skills arena bring congratulations. Emily's first attempts at spaces draw Mrs. Evertson's attention. It is so important for children to receive support for their breakthroughs. Also, no one pushed her to create additional spaces on this, her first day to venture into spaces.

The children, at their tables, watch and listen when the adults confer with someone nearby, and Frederick saw and heard Mrs. Evertson's comments—and Emily's excitement—about her spaces between words.

Mrs. Evertson, however, waits to teach Frederick about spaces on a day she sees him engaged in what, to him, is a great piece of writing. Then she simply suggests to him that he add more information. And he does—plus, he initiates the possibility of a space. That proves to be harder than he intended, but Frederick is undaunted. His energy is high!

This attention to exactly what each child needs is invaluable. So is the time they have to write. Importantly, in this classroom, the children never have to give up time by standing in line waiting for help from the teacher; their teachers are always among them.

What This May Mean for Your Classroom

Some of you may be saying, "I have my students write on lined paper to help them focus on how they place their words."

Many primary-grade teachers use story paper—the type of paper with lines at the bottom and blank space at the top—to encourage their students to use both letters and pictures in their drafts. Actually, this type of paper tends to limit young writers and is not particularly helpful as they develop their spatial awareness when writing. The blue lines printed on story paper can often be a visual distraction, as well as a physical distraction to your young writers. They have to try hard to move those little hands in a way that keeps the print on those lines, so another physical task, such as creating spaces, may get pushed aside.

In addition, many of your young writers need lots of white space to experiment with different types of writing, including maps, vignettes with short bits of dialogue captured in "talking bubbles," or larger-scale drawings with labels. These genres often require smaller strings of text, and allow your writers to think about their words individually. And, as many of your young writers will tell you, it is nearly impossible to recreate a video game screen (complete with the "pows" and "bams" and other various sound effects) on story paper!

Some of you may be saying, "A few of my students can read fairly well, so I know they have a concept of word, but when they write, they still don't leave spaces between words."

Young writers bubbling with ideas often find it difficult to slow down their hand movements enough to put in those spaces. They get caught up in their story or are afraid they won't get a particularly important part onto the page if they slow down! Using a finger is awkward, and lifting the pencil and slightly scooting the hand across the paper is an act that only becomes natural over time.

When your children create a few lines of text without spaces, the draft, however, becomes difficult for them to reread. Over what is usually a short period of time, with your support, they will realize they need to change their strings of letters.

Some children develop their own strategies until leaving spaces becomes more automatic. Jenesse Evertson's six-year-old son, Joe, recently showed her his latest strategy to help him with rereading his longer stories. After a few months of struggling with spacing on story paper at school, he came to his mum with several sheets of plain white printer paper covered from top to bottom with what appeared to be dashes. When his mother asked him to tell her about them, he replied, "These are for my words!" Each dash represented what may become a word for the story he was set to write. He had created a strategy to set each word off so he wouldn't have trouble rereading later!

Some of your young writers will reach a point when they want to move forward, and then they will experiment with strategies of their making. You can support them by recognizing their efforts first, celebrating their cleverness and giving them space to fully explore that strategy, and then, in time, teaching them more conventional approaches to spacing.

Closing Thought

Young writers' concept of word emerges as they experiment with spaces. They see and talk about special words in the books adults read to them, and talk about words with the other writers and adults at the tables where they write. Gradually, as they hear and write the first and ending sounds of words and reread their writing, they start to include the spaces they need in order for their exact meaning to be clear.

CHAPTER 5

We Teach Our Writers to Use Various Spelling Strategies

Young writers not only focus their attention on spaces—they wonder, of course, about the letters in the words they want to use. They practice their budding knowledge of sound-symbol correspondences, and they use classroom resources to spell some words conventionally. Gradually, young writers use a variety of understandings as they learn to spell—including their realization that they can't easily read their work unless they work on their spelling.

Snapshot of Mari
A Kindergarten Writer

In a kindergarten classroom at the school where Holly Tower taught, young Mari begins her daily writing. She shows her comfort level with her classroom routine by quietly choosing, from the shelf of various kinds of paper, a sheet with space for drawing and lines for printing. The choice of paper with lines is a signal of her intent to use words in her writing today.

Next, Mari sits with her usual mixture of five students, and chooses an aqua crayon from the cup on the table. She is ready to work. Mari draws two figures, and around them, a red line. Then she draws herself in bed, and completes that part of her drawing with an orange square.

At this point, Mari faces Ms. Tower, the literacy specialist in her classroom. Ms. Tower is sitting at Mari's table, beside Mari, and Mari offers an explanation of her writing process, "I thought about this last night. I thought about it last night and now I am doing prewriting."

Mari grabs a brown crayon and makes a square around her entire illustration, as if enclosing her work in a frame.

Then she turns the paper over and draws two figures dressed in black, both smiling. One wears a dress, the other, pants. The figure in pants seems to be doing a cartwheel, with excitement rainbows shooting out of his feet.

"I like doing prewriting," Mari explains to Ms. Tower.

Ms. Tower nods, smiles, and asks, "What's your plan, Mari? What's your next step?"

"I am gonna do the writing part now," says Mari, slowly. "I will use my lines."

"What are you going to say?"

"Just what it says in the picture," Mari says, "but I will use letters for this part."

"Tell me what it says in the picture, Mari."

"Well, the first part will say *I went to my Grandma's house with Mrs. Conti.*"

The two of them confirm the previous evening's fun event, and then Mari begins to "use letters."

She labors carefully over each letter in *went*, repeating each sound several times with her hand on her chin, as she has seen her teacher and Ms. Tower do during mini-lessons. Confident, she does not request help.

When she gets to the word *my* she says, "I know that word, it's my sight word, M-Y."

She then labors over *grandma's, house,* and repeats *with* several times, trying to decide how to represent it, settling on a *Y*. Again, confident, Mari does not request help, and Ms. Tower quietly watches, learning about this writer.

Then, pointing to a word card across the room, Mari says, "See, Mrs. Conti. Her name's spelled right up there!" Mari gets up with her paper and pencil, walks to the side of the room, and copies *Mrs* from the card on the wall (omitting the period).

Full of energy, Mari returns to her table, and writes *Coti* on her own.

"I went to my Grandma's house with Mrs. Conti."

Now, she turns over her sheet of paper, ready for the second part of her day's work. "*My* again! Sight word!" Mari is clearly happy with the words she can spell effortlessly.

"*My* what, Mari?" asks Ms. Tower.

"*My parents went to a party*, like the prewriting says," Mari replies, and continues to use a combination of her memory and the repetition of sounds over and over, finding letter by letter, until her sentence is done:

"My parents went to a party."

What This Writer Can Do: Strengths and Breakthroughs

- Mari knows many sound-symbol correspondences she can use to represent words. Importantly, with Ms. Tower beside her, Mari confidently stretches her words to hear the sounds, and writes the letters as she hears them. In their mini-lessons, her teachers have devoted much time to this process of stretching out words, and she knows what to do. Mari asks for no assistance.

- Mari has started to learn her own set of sight words, and recognizes them when she needs one. "Sight word!" she exclaims, and writes the word in conventional spelling. After a child can read a word in context, their teachers provide the child with a small card, and Mari keeps her treasured set in a small Sight Word box of "Words I Know." Importantly, again, even though Ms. Tower sits beside her, Mari confidently writes her sight words. She asks for no assistance.

- Mari uses resources in the classroom, such as Mrs. Conti's name card, when she needs these words in her writing. Her teacher places word cards as labels in various places in her classroom and demonstrates for the children, within her mini-lessons, possible uses of them in their writing. Mari knows how to do this, and writes her entire piece of writing without asking for assistance. This kindergarten girl is an independent writer.

Snapshot of Abbey

A First-Grade Writer

We now move up to Grade 1, to revisit the classroom in which Charles turned us grown-ups from squares into rectangles. On the day of our current snapshot, however, we have stepped back in time. It is the twelfth day of school, and the children are scattered all over the floor, with their writing from day one until now—12 days' worth—spread around them.

The children's task, as demonstrated by Ms. O'Connor in her mini-lesson, is to look at their collections of writing in order to figure out what they can do now that they couldn't do when they started first grade.

Over in one corner of the classroom sits Abbey with her stack of writing in her lap. She holds one piece of paper at a time directly in front of her face, moves her lips, slides her head back and forth, and then places each one upside down to form a neat pile beside her.

Researcher Jane Hansen sits near Abbey, but can't hear what she is saying. When Abbey has placed all of her writing upside down beside her, she stands, looks Mrs. Hansen in the eye, and states, matter-of-factly, "I can't read any of it." And, then, with determination, she adds, "I'm going to write something I can read."

With intention she walks to a table where a few other children have started to gather, sits, and Mrs. Hansen joins them. Abbey draws an *M*, crosses it out, slowly says *Dear* a few times, and writes: *DRA*. She repeats this process for *Miss Mowry* and *How*.

This is a lot of work, and she asks the boy beside her how to spell, "was your birthday?" He misunderstands, and writes: *is your* on Abbey's paper. At this point Mrs. Hansen steps in, "I think Abbey would like to write this note by herself. Is that true, Abbey?" Abbey smiles and nods.

Mrs. Hansen helps her get back into her task, by stretching out the word *birthday* with her. Then Abbey takes off on her own, printing one letter/number for each of the next few words. She knows how to spell *me*. Next, Abbey rereads for Mrs. Hansen, and realizes the word *you* is missing, so she squeezes it in.

"Dear Miss Mowry
How was your birthday? One day can you eat with me?
I love you, Miss Mowry."

Then, as if an explanation is in order, Abbey says, "I decided to write a note to Miss Mowry so she can read it." Aha! Abbey couldn't read any of her writing, so she decided to write a note to Miss Mowry. What better reason to write something readable than to write a note you can actually give to someone? Miss Mowry is their beloved classroom instructional aide, and it was her birthday yesterday. The children had created cards for her, which was great fun.

Abbey finishes her note, takes it to Miss Mowry, who puts her arm around little Abbey and says, "This looks very special, Abbey. Will you read it to me, please?" Abbey does! Miss Mowry keeps the note, and Abbey skips to her table.

What This Writer Can Do: Strengths and Breakthroughs

- Abbey makes a deliberate decision to spell words so she can read her writing. To slow down, stretch out words, listen for sounds, and write the corresponding letters is a painstaking task—but she decides it is worth doing. Her teacher's directive to find evidence of her growth brought this young writer to take herself seriously. She no longer dashes of strings of letters and then "reads" them back by telling a story about a giant, as happened on a previous day when Mrs. Hansen conferred with Abbey.

- Abbey knows many sound-symbol correspondences, and can spell the sight word *me*. She can insert a word when her rereading reveals one is missing, and she can read her note to Miss Mowry!

- Abbey can choose a genre that requires her to write something she needs to read. She created an authentic writing task for herself. She knows that writing for someone else, rather than for herself, will keep her focused on her new goal. Abbey is an astute young writer.

What the Teachers Do

Mari's kindergarten teacher and the literacy specialist provide instruction in how to use various spelling resources so the children can use that knowledge as they learn to write.

Ms. Tower, a resource teacher, and Ms. Hartwell, the classroom teacher, provide instruction during the writing workshop, and Ms. Hartwell reinforces literacy skills throughout the day. They teach the children sound-symbol correspondences every day in order to foster their independence as writers.

This instruction occurs at various times. Typically, one of the settings is when either teacher demonstrates her writing process in a mini-lesson before the children go to their tables to create their own compositions. As the adult composes a message, the class says the letters they hear as the teacher sounds out the words. Early in the year, when Ms. Tower wrote about her son, Sam, the children provided the first and final letter while Ms. Tower provided the vowel. Later in the year, the children provided that as well.

In addition to sounding out words, the teachers show the children how to use various resources posted around the room, such as names, colors, and months. Plus, the children look for words they remember hearing in their favorite books. The picture books their teachers read and reread to the class sit in prominent places and provide many words the children can find when they want them.

Also, after a child can read a word in context, their teachers write the word on a little card, and each child possesses a collection of their own sight words they keep in a handy plastic container.

Overall, when it is time to write:

- Mari's kindergarten teachers expect her and her classmates to figure out how to spell words as best they can.

- These teachers do not see the words for which children write their own spellings as misspellings. Instead, these words are considered representations of what the children know and what the teachers will eventually teach.

- There is no such thing as a misspelled word in this class.

Abbey's first-grade teacher teaches her young writers to evaluate their progress and set goals that will lead them forward as writers.

This is an important process, and Abbey's teacher, Elaine O'Connor, asks the children to periodically engage in a version of what we saw on the day of our snapshot of Abbey. As the children spread throughout the room, they determine various goals to pursue, and Abbey decides she wants to be able to read her work, which leads her into her first concentrated effort to spell.

The children in Ms. O'Connor's class vary tremendously, and Abbey was one of the few whose writing appeared as strings of letters. Usually, her first few letters resembled words she wanted to use to begin her text and then she appeared to fill that first line and another two or three lines with random letters.

For Abbey, learning to make letters was new and fun! To her, writing was mainly a time to practice these new creations.

Our snapshot, however, shows a turning point. Everyone is reading their work to clusters of classmates, but Abbey appears to know she can't do that. She hides behind her papers as she seemingly tries to read them.

Before anyone says anything to her, she announces her intention and heads toward the shelf of various kinds of paper Ms. O'Connor has available. Then, Abbey composes at a table of children with varied expertise, another aspect of their writing workshop that her teacher ensures—so the children can learn to help each other. Abbey soon reaches the point where she usually gives up and just finishes lines with letters. On this day, however, she knows she can't do that. If she does, she won't be able to read this important note.

So she asks for help. This is a wise move but, unfortunately, her tablemate has yet to learn how to help Abbey stretch out words. Mrs. Hansen makes a mental note to mention this to Ms. O'Connor so she can provide another mini-lesson on this hard-to-learn skill, and then Mrs. Hansen quietly redirects Abbey, who carefully, slowly, sounds out every word for the remainder of her note—at least the first letter.

Ms. O'Connor has observed that the key to releasing children who are mired in the difficulties of writing is to create a setting in which they are engaged in a task they *want* to do well. In Abbey's case, she wants to be able to read what she writes, and our snapshot of her shows how much effort it takes for her to spell. But, persist she does. This note must be readable; the time it takes to dwell on each word becomes worthwhile.

Abbey starts to move forward as a young writer who is willing to focus on spelling—as well as on *what* she wants to say.

Overall, Ms. O'Connor:

- trusts her students to know what they need to do next in order to become better writers.

- teaches her students to reread their writing in order to find out if the words are all in order—and all present.

- realizes the importance of her students' daily practice, during writing, as they use the sound-symbol correspondences she teaches them in reading.

- does not let children confuse good writing with good spelling.

Writer-Friendly Classroom Features

Mari's Kindergarten Classroom

If you had walked into this classroom on the day Mari wrote about her parents going to the party, you would have found yourself in a writing workshop that began months earlier on the first day of kindergarten.

Typically, the children plan their writing ahead of time—sometimes the previous evening—as Mari did. They know they will write every day and they know it is their responsibility to be ready—as is the habit of real writers. And they *are* real writers.

Mari and the other children often create drawings as rehearsal for the words they will place on their writing. We are careful to note, however, that for many young writers, and even older ones, drawing is not a rehearsal, but integral to the draft as we saw in Chapter 1. Although Mari may consider this "prewriting," we can see from her picture that the "excitement rainbows" give additional meaning and insight into her draft. Mari is just beginning to realize how text conveys meaning; she conveys important aspects of her meaning via her pictures. Mari easily draws her figures. Then it is time to figure out those words!

While Mari writes her narrative, other children are busily engaged, also, in the writing workshop. At any moment, you can hear someone talking about a game at recess, someone else about nocturnal animals (their current content area of study), another child asking a friend for the "letter" of /th/. You can see two girls at a chart with their writing in hand, and two boys sit—sharing a book—with their writing on the floor beside them. You realize you are amid workers in their writing workshop. You open your notebook, uncap your pen, and begin to take notes.

As in the snapshot of Mari, the teachers spend their time among the children while they write. They learn about the children's writing processes and the content they are writing about. Plus, of course, they nudge them forward as writers.

Importantly, the children look forward to writing, enjoy it, and they know their teachers are interested in what they are doing!

Abbey's First-Grade Classroom

On this particular day, the children in Ms. O'Connor's class were evaluating themselves as writers for the first time, and they were enjoying revising their work. Although Abbey studies each of her pieces of writing by herself with a worrisome seriousness, other children view this task as an opportunity for celebration, "Listen to this! I wrote about my brother and I couldn't spell his name!" "Look! I drew and drew and drew aaaall this, and I hardly wrote anything!" The room resounds with voices of excitement.

Then, gradually, the children start to put their collections into a yellow contact-paper covered box in which they keep their oversized folders of writing. Ms. O'Connor has an orange box ready with a new set of folders for the next several weeks.

As they start to write, if you move among them, some of the children will tell you they are working on something new they have not yet tried as a writer, such as one boy who decided to learn to use exclamation marks—something a child in his cluster on the floor was excited about in his writing.

Several children see this as a regular writing day; they have started new pieces of writing with no particular goal in mind—they have an idea and this is the time to put it on paper. You may hear Ms. O'Connor as she confers with some of these young writers, including a girl who included four of her sight words in her new draft, some of them spelled correctly and some not! Ms. O'Connor confers with the child about the information in her writing, always mindful to pay attention to what the writer wants to say. Then, Ms. O'Connor asks the young writer to check her sight words. It is important for the children to practice their reading skills when they write.

Other children have drafts from their folders in front of them, to which they have decided to insert letters into words, sometimes because their sound-symbol knowledge has improved, and sometimes because they now know how to use their word wall. They are learning to spell—and they are intent on practicing it right now.

What This May Mean for Your Classroom

Some of you may be saying, "Shouldn't I correct my students' misspellings?"

No. Children learn to spell through a process of trial and error as they work to write in contexts that are meaningful for them. Your children will learn and apply their knowledge of letter sounds and spelling conventions as they experiment within their own writing for their own, self-selected purposes.

As your young writers learn to use the tools around them, they will create and revise hypotheses about writing and spelling. Conventional spelling becomes important as they learn that their writing is important and serves real purposes. Importantly, as your children decide to construct messages that they want others to read, they will work diligently to sound out letters and use their collections of known words.

You will respond to their content and honor their attempts to form words, just as you respond to their intent when they speak. You surround your students with an environment where spoken words serve a purpose, and you provide them with a rich environment filled with the many ways they use print in their lives. Similarly, you teach the many ways writers can figure out how to spell words, which helps your children to learn what spelling is, does, and means in their lives as writers.

Some of you may be saying, "Is a child who relies on sight words really an independent writer?"

Our young writers need and deserve the truth from us as we know it. Writers use tools. It is something that all writers do. For us, as adults, tools such as a computer and spell-check are common and facilitate our compositions. Why wouldn't we use them? Similarly, you will teach your young writers to use the resources that are available to them.

Sight word cards, personal dictionaries, labels around the classroom, and peers can and should be used as they apply to the meaningful, real-world situations and curriculum that your students will write about.

Learning to spell is not just sounding out words, and it is more than memorizing sight words. It involves figuring out how to apply the rules gleaned from seeing, hearing, and doing things with words. Children discover and apply these rules in authentic contexts and find out what works and what doesn't.

Some of you may be saying, "In our division/school/classroom, we correct our students' misspellings by writing the correct spelling over it. Why not continue this?"

Children have told us, in various ways, and sometimes quite forcefully, "If you write on my paper, it is no longer my paper." Remember Quandra in Chapter 1?

Children do not learn to spell by having your wealth of knowledge and experience poured on top of their efforts, they learn to spell by developing and extending knowledge about letters and sounds. They use what they know and take risks to learn more.

A very grave danger is that by crossing out their "incorrect" spelling and writing the "correct" spelling over it, children will learn that their attempts are not valued. They will begin to think that their important work of communicating through writing is not where they should direct their energy. When conventional spelling is more important than learning to *use* spelling, children may limit themselves to only the words they are confident they can spell correctly.

Some of you may be saying, "Our division/school/team sets writing goals for students. We need to emphasize those."

Real writers develop goals for themselves. When your children care deeply about their learning and writing and are engaged in writing for self-selected and authentic purposes, they will work to improve, set goals, and evaluate their progress. Very often part of the basis for their self-evaluation reflects what they see as valued within the writing and learning community you will create.

In a literate classroom community, what is valued comes from what you expose your children to throughout the day. You, as the teacher, can set up a language- and literacy-rich environment in which your students interact with materials that reflect state and division standards and, at the same time, you can allow them the freedom (which they'll take anyway) of bringing themselves—and what they value—into their learning process.

Closing Thought

Young writers' knowledge and use of spelling develops in a variety of ways simultaneously. They use their knowledge of letters and sounds to develop spellings, they develop a store of known sight words they can use when they write, and they use books and environmental print to help them spell familiar words that are beyond their letter-sound and sight-word knowledge. Their evaluations of their work can increase their interest in spelling.

CHAPTER 6

We Teach Our Writers the Purposes of Periods

One of the challenges our young writers face when they want to revise and finesse their work is how to use periods. Those little dots fascinate them! The children quickly learn to automatically put a period at the end of a thought when they write only one idea. They also learn to put periods at the end of every line when each thought lives on a separate line. When they learn to create sentences that stop and start mid-line, trouble arrives. Eventually, they start to figure out where to place periods in order for their messages to be clear and readable to others.

Understanding how to control periods is challenging; the notion of where to begin and end sentences does not follow definite rules. Children gradually acquire a concept of *sentence* as they write frequently, gain experience with different forms of writing, and write about ideas and topics in which they have a keen interest. In the upcoming snapshots, we see three first-grade children as they progress through the possibilities of periods.

A First-Grade Writer

For several days at the very beginning of the school year, the first-grade children in Elaine O'Connor's classroom wrote about topics of their choice every day, and Ms. O'Connor used those days to become acquainted with her new students. Many of them wrote short narratives about what they did outside of school, such as this example by Charles, the boy you met in Chapter 1 when, later in the year, he wrote his riddle about the rectangles and squares. This is a narrative Charles wrote on one of his first days of first grade:

"I watch TV with my mom."

The day he wrote this was also one of the two days each week when Jane Hansen, the researcher in their classroom, came to interact with the children, record notes, and observe. While Charles wrote she watched him talk to himself, write *tV*, talk to himself, draw the square, talk to himself, write the *M*, and close with a flourishing, floating, final period; next, he drew.

Then, Jane asked Charles to read his writing to her, and he said, "I watch TV with my mom." In his illustration, we see Charles and his mom watching TV, a favorite pastime for the two of them.

When the children's early writing consisted of only one thought, and they did not intend to write more, Ms. O'Connor taught them to place a period at the end. A period tells your readers that you are finished. Periods play an important role in creating conventional writing that others can effectively follow and read.

What This Writer Can Do: Strengths and Breakthroughs

- Charles can write a sentence and end it with a period. When he reads his print, he reads it as a perfect sentence, even though he is not yet ready to write all the words. When we listen to him, we know he understands how print works. This is a complete, important thought, and he can tell you more about watching TV with his mom if you ask him what they watched the previous evening. He has written all he intends to write, however, and he tells you so with his period.

- Charles knows print moves from left to right. This is a huge accomplishment, and one that young writers all learn, even though many of them begin their use of print by placing individual letters beside key elements in their drawings, such as an *m* beside a drawing of their mom. The period is an early form of punctuation for the children to use, and its use helps them to realize the directionality of print.

Snapshot of Roger

Another First-Grade Writer

Two weeks into the school year, Ms. O'Connor thinks her new writers can move beyond the brief thoughts many of them write, so she plans a mini-lesson. As the children gather around her, she engages them in a conversation about the lunchroom. As Mrs. Hansen listens, she begins to sense that the children have sometimes engaged in a bit of rambunctious behavior while eating. So, Ms. O'Connor has cleverly developed a mini-lesson to encourage her writers to write longer texts—and behave in the lunchroom!

She begins, "Today when you write, you are each going to write a list of the rules you think are important for the lunchroom. Who knows what a *list* is?" The children point out various lists in the classroom, such as the list of *What We Do in the Hall*.

Then, Ms. O'Connor asks, "What are some of your ideas for lunchroom rules?" They have lots! "Be good." "Don't hit anybody!" "Sit still." "Don't yell." The children's ideas continue, and Ms. O'Connor closes the mini-lesson with what we come to regard as her instructional mantra, "Try to write something you think no one else will write."

As they settle at their tables to write, Mrs. Hansen notices Roger. Many of the children chat as they settle in, but Roger doesn't say much. He carefully draws the stools the children sit on at their lunch table and then he draws a child with an extended hand, offering a cookie to another child, whom he labels Brittany.

Then, with little hesitation, Roger lists four rules, reads his list to himself, and adds a third child to his drawing:

"Don't share lunch ("cookie" in illustration)
Don't throw food on the floor
Don't spill on purpose
Don't kick kids"

Interested in the addition to his drawing and the list of rules, Mrs. Hansen photocopies his draft (above). Unable, however, to decipher some of it, Mrs. Hansen initiates a conversation, "Roger, please tell me about your drawing."

"This is Karlene and she is sharing a cookie with Brittany. This, I don't know who this is, but he fell sleep at lunch. We're not s'posed to do that."

Mrs. Hansen extends the conversation about the drawing, and then says, "Please read your rules to me." Roger does.

They talk about his interesting rules, and then Mrs. Hansen says, "I think there is something writers usually put at the end of each rule so readers know that one rule is over and a new rule will begin on the next line." No problem. Roger immediately understands her hint and quickly supplies periods.

When the children wrote only one idea, they ended it with a period, but now, with the goal of writing more, it seems Roger's many ideas consumed his attention, and he and some of his classmates temporarily forgot all about periods.

When young writers try something new, they often temporarily forget their former skills. A quick reminder from Mrs. Hansen, however, instantly brought periods to Roger's list.

Snapshot of Kasandra

Another First-Grade Writer

It is February and the class studies several American heroes, including Abraham Lincoln and Martin Luther King, Jr. Ms. O'Connor reads several books to her students and they become engrossed in the lives of these fascinating historical figures. Plus, these six-year-olds relate to the lives of the historic figures in personal ways, and they mingle the historical lives with their own. Importantly, their writing reveals their complex thinking, as we will hear in Kasandra's essay.

Also, we will see what happens when the children write longer texts. The simplicity of placing a period at the end of each line disintegrates when one sentence follows another on a line, such as happens in some of their writing at this time of the year. Even though Ms. O'Connor has been showing the children how to replace the word *and* with a period, and has been reminding them to do so, this is a complicated task.

Here is an essay Kasandra wrote (Hansen, 2005) toward the end of their study of famous Americans:

"President loves us."

Aberhamliining was a prasindent for the unninnit state of amarce he uostto keep the black peple safe and Aberhamlining and the black peple woer tems togather like the white peple woer atach to the black peple the black peple and the white peple hate each

"Abraham Lincoln was a president for the United States of America. He used to keep the black people safe, and Abraham Lincoln and the black people were teams together, like the white people were attached to the black people. The black people and the white people hated each"

(continued below)

other the black had to give thair set to the white peple and the black peple was made at the white peple if the black peple had fite the white peple the black peple wotif had being in jell and maybe the white peple wotif had came to tees the black peple.

"other. The black had to give their seat to the white people, and the black people was mad at the white people. If the black people had fight the white people, the black people would have had been in jail and maybe the white people would have had come to tease the black people."

Kasandra, as a first-grade student, understands the complexity of our nation's history for her African American race and for white people. Plus, she knows about Abraham Lincoln's legacy. But, she places him on a bus from the era of Martin Luther King, Jr.!

When Mrs. Hansen and Kasandra talk about her essay, Mrs. Hansen asks Kasandra about the attacks and teasing, and Kasandra explains that she watched a movie at home. She has captured in writing some of what she saw in the movie.

Ms. O'Connor is impressed by what Kasandra knows—and by her ability to express herself in this essay, even though her complex thinking does not necessarily break itself into easy-to-decipher thoughts, nor easy-to-read sentences. When Mrs. Hansen tells Kasandra that she can probably add a period to her seventh line, Kasandra rereads the surrounding text and figures out, on her own, where to place the period. Her text will now be easier to understand, and she will learn to reread her drafts with the possibility of adding periods to clarify her meaning.

When Kasandra wrote simpler essays, she could separate her thoughts with periods, but now, as when Roger jumped from one-line writing to four—and his use of periods temporarily vanished—Kasandra will start to relearn her ability to use periods. Using periods to punctuate and separate sentences is more challenging within the complex thoughts she now tries to convey in print.

In the throes of intense writing, it is easy for young writers to not think about periods. Indeed, temporarily dropping known skills as they take on new ones often leads to spurts of growth (rather than a steady, gradual increase), a common pattern of developmental growth for young—and older—writers.

For the remainder of the year, Ms. O'Connor continues her mini-lessons as gentle reminders to her students to insert periods, and they respond. They learn to reread their writing and, gradually, they insert periods more regularly.

What These Two Writers Can Do: Strengths and Breakthroughs

- Roger and Kasandra have written their longest pieces of writing to date. Roger understands the notion of a sentence; he demonstrates his understanding by starting each lunchroom rule on a new line. Kasandra creates a long essay in which sentences stop and start mid-line.

- Both children, when reminded, know where to place periods. No adult inserts periods into these students' writing! The children do it themselves—with hints from adults who circulate among them while they write.

- Kasandra and Roger, after writing their longest pieces of writing ever, realize they have gained fluency and continue to write longer pieces of writing. For Roger, his teacher challenged him to write more than one line, and he quickly wrote four. For Kasandra, her own strong emotions brought her to the page with much to say and she said it—and in a forceful voice, too!

What the Teacher Does

Ms. O'Connor maintains her focus and that of her first-grade children on the content they are writing about, so they learn the purpose of periods is to clarify their information.

At the beginning of the year, when many of the children wrote only one simple thought, Ms. O'Connor taught them to place a period at the end of that thought. This was relatively easy for the young writers. Basically, these periods told their readers: I am finished.

Then, when the children wrote longer pieces of writing, with one thought per line, she taught them to put a period at the end of each line, not just at the very end of a piece of writing. Some of the children continued to write this way for quite some time; indeed, they wrote narratives, stories, and reports—one sentence per line.

A few children, however, noticed that the books she read to them do not have periods at the end of every line, so Ms. O'Connor invited them to extend their thoughts beyond the ends of lines and start new thoughts mid-line. Often, however, it is difficult to know exactly when one thought ends and the next begins. Periods mid-line are difficult for young writers, and Ms. O'Connor is careful to maintain their focus on *what* they say, so they don't worry about periods.

Ms. O'Connor, who has taught them from the beginning of the year to reread their texts, now needs to re-emphasize this. Often, it is when the children reread their texts, and have difficulty doing so, that they realize the importance of a period to clarify their own meaning.

Overall, Ms. O'Connor maintains the focus on the content of what the children write, and gently suggests the addition of periods in locations the young writers can identify. Gradually, the young writers learn why and when periods matter.

Ms. O'Connor teaches the use of periods within the children's writing.

These first-graders are personally invested in their writing; they want to convey what they mean, and they want their readers to appreciate their thoughts. So, they gradually learn to use periods to their advantage.

Given that they write four times a week, they have many opportunities to gain fluency, and Ms. O'Connor has many opportunities within this time frame to teach them about periods. She always does so by inviting them to add periods within their own work. Ms. O'Connor does not give the children worksheets on which they find text written by others for them to punctuate. They have their own daily writing, and they learn about periods within writing they care deeply about and want to be able to share with others.

Overall, Ms. O'Connor teaches her students about periods when she:

- reads aloud to them, pointing out the different ways in which book authors end their sentences.

- demonstrates with her own writing, thinking out loud as she writes and making comments about the punctuation she chooses to use—why she chooses a particular punctuation mark and how she determines to use it to accomplish a specific purpose.

- celebrates well-placed periods in a classmate's writing as the classroom author reads his writing to the class.

Writer-Friendly Classroom Features

If you had walked into this classroom periodically throughout the year you would have seen, on any given day, children using periods—and other ending punctuation—in nearly every way possible. On any particular day you could see multiple genres and writing formats being pursued by various children: lists, stories, letters, poetry, and research reports—and the children would be placing periods at the end of their writing, at the ends of the lines, mid-line, or nowhere—depending on the child and on the task. All of them are focused on transferring what is in their heads onto the paper; most likely, none of them focus on periods.

Over time, however, you will hear, in their conversations while they write, questions about periods. And you will hear Ms. O'Connor remind them of the glory of periods and what helpful guideposts they provide for readers. As with spelling, the children gradually gain expertise and will continue to learn about and refine these skills.

As you may remember, this is the classroom in which, on two days each week, the children write about whatever they want in whatever genre they choose. And, on two days, Ms. O'Connor provides a general topic in line with a classroom line of study and/or a particular genre for them to try. These varied experiences with topics and genres help to encourage the children's experiments with and uses of periods.

What This May Mean for Your Classroom

Some of you may be saying, "I have always inserted periods onto my children's writing to show them where they belong."

Yes, what you do is very common. You will now, however, give that responsibility to your young writers. With you beside them, they will add their own periods. Their writing belongs to them. The thoughts, words, and periods are theirs.

When their writing needs periods you will talk with them about where periods could go, and most likely they will be able to figure out where to put one or two. One or two is most likely enough for a young learner to add—they gradually learn about periods. They don't learn everything about them within one piece of writing!

Also, something important you will also notice is that as your writers start to understand how periods work, you will hear their table-talk focus, at times, on these important dots. They will ask their friends about sentences and engage in conversations about where they think periods belong. You will learn a great deal about what they know as you listen in on these conversations. Sometimes, of course, you will join their talk—and they will appreciate your suggestions and comments.

Some of you may be saying, "In my school division we have a rubric, and young children's use of periods receives more weight than their expression."

Yes, that is the case in some school divisions where, unfortunately, uninformed persons have created the rubric. You, however, want your writers to end their sentences with correct punctuation AND write with expression. It belies the nature of children to not place emphasis on the strength of their thoughts and feelings. Your young writers feel deeply about certain things, and you know this because of what you see when you watch them interact with each other. It is wrong for their ways with words to not count when they have a piece of paper in front of them.

It is natural for children to write with strong feelings. They frequently express intense responses throughout their daily lives, and they hear you read about characters with deep emotions when you read to them each day. You read with lively expression, and your writers relish the words of the professional writers who author the children's literature you and your children use as mentor texts. You want your young writers to be able to say, "I am a writer!" and central to that role is their desire to emulate the writers you share with them every day.

Some of you may be saying, "I'm afraid I don't usually ask my writers about what they are saying before I bring up periods."

You have learned to think that good writing is printed neatly, punctuated properly, and spelled correctly. Now, however, you no longer buy into that simplistic view of writing. Your writers want you to look inside their writing, just as you look inside them when you listen to them as they talk to you.

It is the intent of the messenger that speaks at you first. Only after the intent is understood do the periods matter.

Importantly, at that point, periods count a great deal. The way you and your children punctuate words clarifies what all of you are trying to say. To learn to finesse a message is the complicated task that periods require of all writers, and it is especially difficult for your young writers who are learning to communicate in clear ways others can easily follow.

Where to place periods is, therefore, not a straightforward task for you to teach. Periods do not follow exact rules. You and your children will find many examples of strings of words that can be punctuated in more than one way. Your discussions about these options will help all of you understand the many purposes periods serve.

Closing Thought

When young writers engage in writing that matters to them, their desire to use periods grows. Gradually, with support from classmates and adults who appreciate their efforts, young writers become increasingly able to use and control periods. At the same time, when children try new genres and more complex tasks, they typically forget what they know about periods. At these times, of course, we step in to remind them of what they know about periods and often they can quickly insert these important, pesky dots. Overall, young writers want their readers to understand what they write; slowly, they learn to use periods to clarify the meaning of their writing.

In these last three chapters, we have focused on some skills young writers need to finesse their work, and now we proceed to the final three chapters of our book. For them we harken back to our very first set of chapters in which we wrote about ways to *engage* young writers. Now, to close, we devote time to what we do to *keep* our children engaged. Most immediately, we return to kindergarten for a look at what the teacher does as she uses evaluation to inform her instruction.

CHAPTER 7

We Use an Evaluation-Instruction Loop

As writing teachers, we constantly watch, listen, and talk with our young writers as they work. This is our main form of evaluation—and a major opportunity for instruction. We always want to know what each child is trying to accomplish. This lets us know what we may do to challenge the child and support his or her forward motion.

We saw in previous chapters how young writers evaluate their own work, sometimes celebrating their accomplishments, and sometimes intentionally pushing themselves forward. Just as evaluation is the constant, ongoing task of a writer, it is also our responsibility as their teachers.

Our continuous evaluations while children write often lead to instant instruction and help us determine what we will teach in subsequent mini-lessons.

Snapshot of Cassie
A Kindergarten Writer

Cassie, a kindergartener in Sue Harris's classroom, stands at the table where she writes, eyeing her open writing book. She then looks at researcher Jenesse Evertson, who is sitting at the table with the children, and announces, "Bodies are made of arms and legs and middles. They have round heads on top. I'll show you mine. Like Mrs. Harris's."

Cassie puts her blue crayon to the paper and begins a narration of her writing/ drawing process, "I'll start with the tops. It's right to start with the tops. Like Mrs. Harris. Then the bodies come off them. Like Mrs. Harris makes lines." She darts Mrs. Evertson a quizzical look, "Can you make lines? I can. See, blue heads and line bodies."

J.T., another writer at the table, leans over to look at Cassie's draft, "Where ya' gonna put the faces?" Cassie replies, "I'll make the heads bigger. Then make the middles like that shape that goes across and up and across and down." She demonstrates with her finger in the air. "A square?" asks J.T. "Yep," says Cassie, "a square."

So Cassie draws one square to try it out; and, then another. She cocks her head to one side and gives her bodies a long, steady look. She squints her eyes doubtfully, pauses, and then swiftly grabs a different crayon and moves it forcefully across and up and down over her draft:

Cassie's scribble-scrabble

"Is this good?" she asks J.T.

J.T. shakes his head. "It's scribble-scrabble."

Later, Mrs. Evertson shows Mrs. Harris Cassie's scribble scrabble and tells her how it came into being. Mrs. Harris, somewhat taken aback, thoughtfully evaluates Cassie's actions.

Mrs. Harris wants Cassie and all of her young writers to value their writing attempts, even if they don't quite match their intentions. Drafts are important; they count. Mrs. Harris knows it is necessary for children just learning to manipulate writing materials to value their efforts. She also knows that young writers will often revisit their drafts at later dates and if they are scribbled-scrabbled over they won't be able to revise them or see their progress as writers.

With all these thoughts whirling in her mind, Mrs. Harris plans her instruction for the next day.

The next morning for her writing demonstration, she uses what she learned from Cassie and from Horn and Giacobbe (2007). Mrs. Harris creates an apple tree, talking through her process as she draws, "I'm starting by drawing a circle in the center of my paper . . . . Now I'm drawing two lines coming down from the circle . . . . Here, at the bottom, I'm adding a few lines that can be roots for my apple tree . . . . Now all my tree needs are apples!" Mrs. Harris picks up a red crayon and draws five gorgeous apples.

As Mrs. Harris draws/writes, Cassie sits very still, face upturned, with her eyes glued to Mrs. Harris. Cassie chimes in with the other children, "Oooh! Aaah!" They all love this tree!

Mrs. Harris then pauses dramatically, picks up a different crayon, and proceeds to scribble all over the page!

The children gasp. Cassie clamps her hand over her mouth! Alexi shouts out in seeming terror, "Why are you scribble-scrabbling?!"

Mrs. Harris thinks aloud, "Maybe I don't think my writing is important . . . is it?"

The children respond with a multitude of passionate *Yeses*. Cassie nods emphatic nods. Briana exclaims, "It's your *writing*!" Then this wise little writer adds, "*Four-year-olds* scribble-scrabble. We are *five*, and we are learning to use our hands." Yes, these children's words echo those they have heard Mrs. Harris speak on previous days.

Cassie looks at Briana and then at her hands; Cassie moves her hands this way and that way, thinking about Briana's words.

Mrs. Harris continues, "Yes, we are learning to use our hands to write and draw. Maybe instead of scribbling over our pictures, we will try again on a new sheet. All of our tries are important."

As the children settle at their tables for their writing time, Cassie announces to Mrs. Evertson, "I'm gonna do a tree today. I'm not gonna scribble-scrabble. I can do trees."

She then begins to draw, narrating her process, "They have tops and middles and bottoms. They have round tops. I make the tops first. And middles. And this bottom what holds them in the ground." She finishes her tree and looks up triumphantly, "Look at the top and bottom!" She then makes some quick vertical and horizontal lines, and some careful wiggly lines off the side, clarifying, "It's NOT scribble-scrabble. I don't DO scribble-scrabble. This is my beautiful tree, ain't it?"

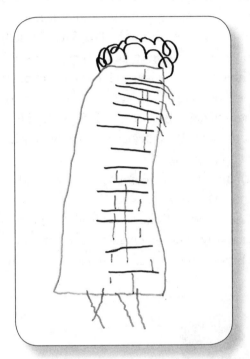

Cassie's tree

What This Writer Can Do: Strengths and Breakthroughs

- Cassie finds value in her teacher's drafts and strives to recreate what she has seen. Even though she wasn't pleased with the circles and squares when she used them to create bodies, she is ready to try again. She follows her teacher's careful lead and experiments with squares and circles in a new way. Critical of her own work, she envisions how her writing should appear and is pleased, "This is my beautiful tree, ain't it?" Cassie is an astute young writer who evaluates her work and tries new ways of bringing her work from her head to her hand.

- Cassie uses another process employed by her teacher—self-narration—to guide her drawing onto paper. Like other young writers, Cassie is using pencils and crayons more frequently since she has started school, but sometimes her hand won't move the crayon exactly the way she intends. How can she control her efforts so she can create work that satisfies her? She decides to talk through her work, just as her teacher demonstrates.

First-Grade Writers

In Elaine O'Connor's first-grade classroom, we see that she and her children use the globe and nonfiction literature to learn about the tilt of our Earth and how this tilt contributes to changes in our weather during the fall. On a Tuesday, one of Ms. O'Connor's days to choose the general writing topic for her class, she invites the children to write about something they have learned in their unit of study.

While they write, researcher Jane Hansen sits at the table where Bristol and Carlene sit, along with two other children. Bristol and Carlene decide to write about the world, and when they start to talk with each other, Bristol writes her title and Carlene writes *The world turns away from the sun.*

Mrs. Hansen confers with them while they compose, and when they talk about the sun with her, they both write: *The sun stays still.*

While the girls continue, their conversation ranges from the globe to the drought their community is currently experiencing. Carlene continues to write about the world and sun, and Bristol creates this two-page draft (Hansen, 2007a):

"The World
The sun stays still.
The world is happy."

The WORlB iS SAD
        Bekz The WorlDrAu
OWt UV WoDR.

*"The world is sad
because the world ran
out of water."*

Carlene also completes her two-page draft:

10·15
10·17

The Worlb turnsaw
Fam The San   and
the San   Sdass saiL

*"The world turns away
from the sun and
the sun stays still"*

> and We Kat Not
> Filit the Wd go a rod the
> San it tacs one day I no hawl the
> Wod gosanTaksis

"and we can not
feel it. The world goes around the
sun. It takes one day. I know how the
world goes on the axis."

At the end of their writing workshop, when Ms. O'Connor studies all of the students' writing, she and Mrs. Hansen (who participates in this examination with Ms. O'Connor once a week) notice the line *The world is happy* in Bristol's draft.

In general, many of the girls in this first grade often write a simplistic line about something being happy. The line doesn't say much. The writer does not seem to have much intention.

Ms. O'Connor and Mrs. Hansen also notice the misunderstanding in Carlene's draft. It takes one *year*, not one *day*, for the world to go around the sun.

Ms. O'Connor decides to invite the two girls to share their drafts from the Author's Chair on Thursday. They use this occasion as the opening experience for their writing workshop for the day, to be followed by time for the class to write. Ms. O'Connor wonders what the children will say in response to the girls' drafts, and what influence the responses may have on the girls as writers. Ms. O'Connor doesn't say anything to either of the girls or the class about why she has chosen them to share. They simply begin.

Bristol reads first. The children, as Ms. O'Connor has taught them, listen for what they can learn from Bristol, and ask questions to learn more—important tasks in writing across the curriculum. Jeremiah picks up on the line *The world ran out of water* and several children, including Bristol, comment on the sanitizing solution they use in their school bathrooms because the custodians turned off the water for the sinks.

Then one child says, "I learned that the world is happy," another child wonders why, and Bristol isn't sure how to answer that.

Ms. O'Connor says, "Maybe Bristol will think about it and add that new information today when we write." The children understand. Ms. O'Connor has been showing them the importance of providing details to clarify their writing; this is not the first mention of that possibility. The children also know Bristol doesn't have to add anything to her draft, but maybe she will. Whether to revise is a decision these first-grade writers make. It is not a decision Ms. O'Connor makes for them.

Now it is Carlene's turn to read her draft to the class. In the conversation that follows, one child repeats what he learned, "We can't feel the world going around." Carlene nods in agreement, stands for a dramatic pause, and says, "I can't feel it!"

Another child says, "I learned that it takes one day to go around the sun." Ms. O'Connor, knowing that these are difficult concepts for the beginning of first grade, carefully reviews the Earth's rotation and annual path around the sun, helping children understand it's a one-year journey, not just a day-long process.

The conversation closes, and the children go to their tables. Each of them decides whether to start a new draft related to their unit of study or continue to work on a draft they have already started.

Bristol chooses to revisit her draft and inserts two pieces of information. After the line *The sun stays still*, she adds *but the world spins*, and after *The world is happy*, she adds *because it is cold.* Evidently, if the world is going to become colder each fall, it must like that!

Carlene does not choose to revisit her draft.

What These Writers Can Do: Strengths and Breakthroughs

- Bristol and Carlene know they can revisit their drafts, and they also know they will not be *required* to "fix" the misinformation because Ms. O'Connor knows that for her to step into their words takes away from their *authority* as writers. These young writers are the ultimate persons responsible for their work, and this keeps their investment high.

- Bristol and Carlene understand that their drafts are not looked at as something that must appear in final form but, rather, serve as reflections of their thinking at a moment in time. Even though Ms. O'Connor specifically designed this mini-lesson

(continued on next page)

as an opportunity to teach them scientific concepts they did not understand, she knows these are complex notions the young children will study repeatedly for years. Bristol, however, does choose to revise her draft, and figures out what she wants to say. Her decision to add information is certainly of her own choosing.

- Bristol and Carlene use responses from others to filter information that is meaningful enough to warrant further exploration on paper. Writing about something they are just beginning to understand is a daunting task; these young writers learn so much in a day that even both sets of fingers couldn't enumerate the new information they take in! So they talk, evaluating what each other says until they find the nuggets they want to use.

What the Teachers Do

Cassie's kindergarten teacher evaluates her young writers and their work in order to plan the instruction she provides in her writing demonstrations.

Mrs. Harris knows Cassie often feels insecure. She entered kindergarten as an interested, verbal child with weak pencil-paper skills and needs to see herself as competent. Determined to help Cassie see herself as a writer from a position of strength, Mrs. Harris created the mini-lesson in which she scribble-scrabbled over her tree—hoping to impress upon Cassie that writers value their drafts.

Also, Mrs. Harris knows that young writers cannot always translate their ideas onto paper. Drawing (and making letters) can be complicated. So what happened when Cassie's intentions didn't correspond to the people she created? In frustration, she cancelled out her draft with scribble-scrabble. Cassie saw her ideas in her head, but she couldn't see them on the page.

Cassie, however, immediately changed her behavior after Mrs. Harris's mini-lesson/writing demonstration. Without using Cassie's name, Mrs. Harris showed and expressed the importance of placing value on their drafts. Cassie quickly understood the gravity of this.

Every day, Mrs. Harris opens their writing workshop by reading literature to the class and creating a piece of writing—her own writing for that day. It is within her writing and the literature that Mrs. Harris provides a great deal of her writing instruction. As often as possible, these lessons are a direct follow-up to something Mrs. Harris has observed her writers doing.

Also, when Mrs. Harris writes in front of the children, she not only talks about her ideas, she vocalizes her actual writing process. The language she uses highlights important pieces of information: direction, form, and shape. Then Cassie narrates her process just as her teacher does. Breaking it down into these fundamental bits makes the big ideas manageable for her.

In addition, Mrs. Harris:

- realizes her children's strengths and capitalizes on them; Cassie was trying to learn how to make some shapes, and Mrs. Harris used those shapes to create a tree—which is easier than drawing people.

- realizes her young writers' physical needs; Cassie, for example, starts to write while sitting on the bench at her table, but is soon standing, intent on her work. Mrs. Harris does not tell her to sit.

- realizes the importance of the children's work; she *never* makes a mark of any kind on the writing of any of her children—and she is teaching them to honor their work as much as she does.

Bristol and Carlene's first-grade teacher evaluates all of her young writers and their work in order to plan instruction.

In this snapshot, we again saw first-grade teacher Elaine O'Connor, whose instructional process is similar to Mrs. Harris in that it is based on her specific evaluations of her children as writers. She confers with them as they write and she studies their work.

In the example of the two girls, some of the instruction occurs within the response the class provides when the girls read their drafts from the Author's Chair. This instruction works because Ms. O'Connor has carefully taught her children to tell the writer what they learn, expand upon it, and ask questions to learn more. Then, as she listens to the children talk, she adds advice and, as needed, she re-teaches.

Overall, Ms. O'Connor's instruction is based on more than one type of evaluation. First, she circulates among the children while they write, peers over their shoulders, and confers with them. Then, because she scheduled writing just before the children's specials classes, they leave their writing on their desks when they leave the room. As she picks it up to put it in their folders, she studies it. Based on her evaluation of what she sees in their work, and what she saw and heard while they were writing, she creates her instructional plans.

In summary: the ongoing teaching-assessment-instruction loop used by Ms. O'Connor and Mrs. Harris is the core of their writing instruction—and the core of the writing instruction for all the teachers in this book.

Writer-Friendly Classroom Features

Cassie's Kindergarten Classroom

If you had walked into Cassie's and Mrs. Harris's kindergarten classroom on the day Mrs. Harris crossed out her tree, you would realize this lesson came from somewhere other than a traditional teachers' manual. Mrs. Harris based her instruction on a scene Jenesse Evertson shared with her, and if she hadn't talked with Mrs. Evertson, Mrs. Harris would have based her instruction on something she had witnessed on her own.

Given her constant interactions with her children as they write, she is able to use what she sees them do as the basis for her instruction. Her instruction, in other words, is directly related to what her students need; it is tailored to meet their specific strengths, needs, and challenges.

Bristol and Carlene's First-Grade Classroom

If you had regularly visited this first-grade classroom you would have been in for a treat on the day Bristol and Carlene read to the cluster of classmates around them. Whereas Mrs. Harris and her kindergarten children closed every writing workshop with an all-class share, Ms. O'Connor's children did not participate in a sharing time each day.

On this day, however, they open their workshop with a sharing time, and you not only enjoy their eagerness during their gathering, you realize they know how to respond to each other. They know what they are doing.

It may have surprised you, however, when the children went to their desks to write, and Carlene did not decide to change her misconception about the earth's revolution in her draft. Ms. O'Connor does not tell her she must. This writing teacher, in other words, knows her instruction is not something each child will use immediately. Carlene knows that writers change their writing—she sees it around her every day. Her friend Bristol is doing it right now. Carlene will revise as well, but with another draft, on another day.

The major aspect of effective evaluation in a classroom of young writers becomes clear in front of our eyes. Ms. O'Connor evaluates/responds to her young writers with one primary goal—to keep their enthusiasm high.

What This May Mean for Your Classroom

Some of you may be saying, "Writing instruction in my school revolves around a curriculum that lists the specific skills we need to teach."

Most schools do follow a curriculum that requires teachers to teach writing specifics throughout the school year and observe young writers for their use of these skills in daily writing or in periodic writing prompts.

But although this list may be perceived as the main thrust of the instruction-evaluation loop, *it is only one piece*. Evaluation in your classroom is constant and ongoing: it occurs when your young writers reread their writing, when they converse with their peers and you, when they listen to other children share their writing, and when you reads books by professional writers. Your young writers evaluate their work and the work of others continually. Meanwhile, the observations you make while your students write, talk, read, and share provide insights that serve as a basis for the instructional decisions that will push your young writers on *at that point in time*.

What this means for your teaching is that you remain *responsive* to your students while keeping the curriculum in mind. Inserting periods, using capital letters, and creating spaces are somewhere on the list of skills you must teach. The chance is very high that all the skills you and your writers engage in are on the list. If there is something on the list that your writers don't try, then you will introduce it to them within your own writing and/or within the children's literature you read.

Keenly observing what your young writers are doing at the present, and then focusing instruction based on their needs, sets the stage for pertinent, responsive instruction, which is the most powerful kind for your children. After all, we doubt you'll find a box in the writing curriculum that addresses scribble-scrabbling! Whether the responsive instruction you provide is one-on-one or for the whole group depends upon the writer(s) and the situation; it requires you to stay attuned to your writers' needs, the needs of the curriculum—and to think beyond just the curriculum.

Some of you may be saying, "I usually consider evaluation as more of a linear process between a teacher and student."

Evaluation involves so much more than a linear process! It is definitely not a one-way street! While you are studying your young writers and considering how to move them forward, they are studying you—your demonstration writing, your responses to their drafts, etc.—and considering how your interactions will influence their ongoing work.

In addition, your young writers keep their ears open to and eyes upon their peers; peer evaluation is a very important aspect of a child's writing experience. Sharing their work in class is one avenue for peer evaluation, and just as important are the conversations your young writers hold with their peers as they write.

Your children are keen to try new things in their drafts, and they continually consider if and how their many and varied interactions will affect their writing. Be sure to consider all the evaluative avenues in your busy class, and recognize how they become integrated into the classroom writing time.

Some of you may be saying, "In our school, evaluation means documenting children's writing growth on a rubric that is based on a midyear writing prompt."

Well, now you know: evaluation is a much broader concept! In relation to required prompts, the drafts produced in response to them, as you already know, often don't convey the understandings of your young writers. Many of them know much more than one piece of writing shows. Plus, writing certainly doesn't proceed in a linear fashion; while a young writer focuses on a particular skill, that same child may completely ignore others!

In relation to the rubric, you are, in various ways, addressing many portions of it on a daily basis. You know whether your children write clear texts, and which ones need more instruction in this area, so you place your attention there when you confer with them and/or in other situations. When your students write every day, you provide daily demonstrations, you all talk about the features of writing in children's literature, and the children know how to learn from others in an all-class share, they will do well when their writing is scored.

What, in addition, does this mean for you as a teacher, given that some of your children will disappoint you on the day they must write to the prompt. You will give your students some practice. They don't need to practice very often, but with a few opportunities interspersed within their choice writing they will quickly learn to write to prompts, which is one of the specific forms of writing in which they must engage.

Also, and very importantly, you will use more than one type of documentation. Your students save their daily writing, you record your conversations, their conversations with each other, and your observations. In general, you use several forms of documentation to provide an insightful portrait of your young writers, and of how you as a teacher have used that insight to help every writer move forward.

Closing Thought

Young writers need an evaluation system that enables them to see value in their work—and in themselves. In order to ensure this, we teachers carefully support them as we show them new possibilities. We evaluate them, their work, and provide instruction the children know is based on what they are doing. This ongoing teaching-assessment loop keeps our young writers engaged in their work as they push themselves forward to learn the best ways to communicate on paper.

CHAPTER 8

We Provide Time for Our Writers to Share with Their Class

Sometimes writers write for themselves but, overall, writers write for audiences. They want to know what their audiences think, and they want to hear other writers. Often they get ideas from others—their classmates, teachers, and professionals. Though children write for a multitude of audiences, it is helpful—and exciting—for them to write for their classmates. Before they share, their teachers provide instruction so the readers know for sure they will be supported. Thus the all-class share is an important aspect of the evaluation of their writing. This way of honoring their work brings the class together and energizes and engages the writers—as does all evaluation of young writers.

Snapshot of Ron Mac
A Kindergarten Writer

Ron Mac is an English language learner in Sue Harris's kindergarten class and appears to speak no English. In his classroom, the same classroom you visited in Chapters 3, 4, and 7, the children write every day. On Fridays they write about a curriculum area they are studying, and on the other four days they write about whatever they want. Ron Mac participates willingly—only willingly, *not* excitedly.

Every day Ron chooses a purple crayon and creates a purple jumble that we adults cannot decipher, and Ron does not tell us, or his classmates, what he is creating. He does begin to talk, and learns to write his name, but every day for an entire semester, yes, for the entire fall of kindergarten, Ron's writing looks very much like this one creation:

Ron's purple jumble

Then, in February, when the class studies Martin Luther King, Jr., Ron amazes himself, us adults, and his classmates! Over a period of days, Mrs. Harris has read several books about Martin Luther King, Jr. to the children, and engaged them in extensive discussions. She then showed a movie about the civil rights leader. It is now time to write. Children may write about whatever they want, and Ron chooses a black marker—a new tool. He uses it to carefully draw three lines of print for his message (Hansen, 2007b).

When it is time for the class to stop writing and gather around the Green Chair—their Author's Chair—for their sharing and response session, Ron holds his writing in front of Mrs. Harris's face. She smiles at him, and his return smile is as wide as his cheeks. Ron wants to share, and he wants to be first! He nestles into the overstuffed chair next to Mrs. Harris and proceeds to read this to the class:

"Be friends. Get on the bus."

That's Martin Luther King, Jr. in a nutshell, and the class claps!

We don't know, of course, exactly what brought Ron to print, but we do know that he made the decision himself.

For the preceding months, however, Mrs. Harris had laid the groundwork. While the children wrote at their tables, she circulated, inviting them to tell her about their writing. She frequently stopped next to Ron; he knew she took note of his work and of him. She expressed interest in his jumbles and hid her worry about his apparent lack of progress. She knows it often takes time for children new to this country to fully participate in a classroom.

The other children at the tables where Ron sat wrote in a more conventional manner—with somewhat realistic drawings and uses of print. He heard them talk as they wrote, watched them create, and they included him in their interactions as much as possible.

Each day, to close their writing time, two or three children shared their writing with the class for response, and Ron willingly joined these gatherings. He appeared interested in what was shared. Never did anyone say anything negative about his own form of participation, which was to smile and watch.

Then, on this February day Ron abandons his purple jumble! He has something important to say, he knows how to draw letters, and he knows how to say the words he wants to say. He is ready!

Yes, he has no sound-symbol correspondences, but he knows what print does. It travels left to right and *it says something important.*

For some children, such as Ron, it is the content the class studies that brings them into writing. They love the curriculum!

The overall climate and the curriculum lead them to make the ultimate decision: *I want to be a writer*.

What This Writer Can Do: Strengths and Breakthroughs

- Ron wants to celebrate his monumental accomplishment by reading it to his classmates; he knows the leap he made today is cheer-worthy! He has seen his classmates—for days, weeks, months—sit in the Green Chair with smiles on their faces, and has heard other children clap and respond. Today he is ready!

- Ron has learned a great deal by listening to and observing the various forms of print and media his teacher uses as part of her instruction. This is evident in the content of his writing and in his use of the Green Chair. It is the place from which children often share their milestones.

- Ron takes many risks on this one day: he uses a different color of crayon, he writes letters from left to right, and he clearly reads his writing to the class. To take any one of these risks in a day would constitute a major breakthrough, and Ron explores all three!

Snapshots of Harrie and Roland

Two Prekindergarten Writers

We now return to the prekindergarten classroom of Robyn Davis, the classroom we visited in our Introduction, and in Chapters 1 and 2. Now, however, we are in the midst of their busy all-class share—in a new format created by Miss Robyn to meet the needs of her diverse class that includes many English language learners.

Instead of the children gathering on the carpet around a classmate who shares from the Author's Chair, all the young writers have placed their writing for the day on their tables, and they are milling around, pulling friends by the hand, pointing to special marks on papers, and chattering excitedly in any one of the six different languages spoken in their class.

Two children from Burma talk quietly about their writing, and a girl who speaks Spanish chats away to a friend who speaks only English—as far as we know.

Nearby, we see Harrie standing beside this piece of his writing:

Harrie's big ol' worm in a big humongous apple

On this particular day, Harrie could not wait to get started on his writing. He knew he had something to tell that his classmates would love! He and his family had just visited a local apple orchard, and Harrie was bursting at the seams with excitement.

Now he has finished and stands beside his writing, waiting for interested lookers, waiting to tell his story.

As a cluster of three gathers around his writing, Harrie starts, "You know what happened up on the really high hill? I found a big ol' worm in a big humongous apple! I was getting ready to take a bite and Mom said, "WAIT, Harrie! Don't eat that big worm!"

Two of the children begin to giggle. Caron says, "Wow, Harrie! I bet you glad your mom saw that worm." Harrie, "Yeh, real glad. 'Cause you know, worms they taste *nasty*." Ruthanne can be quiet no longer, "You know that song we sing? 'Bout the worm in the cupcake? What's 'at song called again?" Both Caron and Harrie exclaim, "*The Yucky Song!*"

Overly excited Caston spins, "One time I ate fifteen zillion worms and they weren't yucky. They were nice. Real nice. My momma she had a fit when she sawed me eat those worms." To this the others respond, "Eeewww!"

At that point, we move across the room to catch another interaction during this all-class share. Miss Robyn, always amazed by her young writers' work, stops beside a child who appears to be quietly waiting—beside this piece of writing:

Roland's Three Bears

Miss Robyn knows this piece of writing belongs to a different child than the one who is standing beside it, so she asks, not knowing if this non-English-speaking child will understand her, "Where is Roland?" The child points, and here comes Roland with a copy of *The Three Bears* book in hand, a book Miss Robyn has read several times to the class.

Hardly acknowledging Miss Robyn's presence, Roland opens the book and talks with excitement in English as he shows illustrations of the bears to his friend. His friend nods, points, and says something in his language, to which Roland responds in English: two languages, one book, two young writers, one piece of writing to bring them together.

What These Writers Can Do: Strengths and Breakthroughs

- Harrie and Roland have learned what will "sell" in a room full of pre-kindergarteners. They write with their upcoming audience in mind. Harrie knows: yucky worms are a great topic! And, Roland knows: everyone in this class loves *The Three Bears*.

- When Harrie and Roland share, they become the teachers in the classroom. Their daily opportunity to tell others about their writing provides them with many, many opportunities to develop their sense of story, to appreciate literature, to become acquainted as writers, and to develop their ability to relate many kinds of text.

What the Teachers Do

Ron's kindergarten teacher created their all-class share to serve many purposes, including opportunities for young writers to share on days when they have tried something brand-new.

Mrs. Harris's young writers gather around their Author's Chair for various reasons. Sometimes a child has written personal news and wants to read it, such as when a child announces a new sibling. Sometimes Mrs. Harris asks a child to share a draft such as when she asked Cassie, the girl in Chapter 7 who drew the "beautiful tree," to explain her work to the class.

At other times, such as we saw with Jamil's Name Hats in Chapter 3 and now with Ron Mac and Dr. Martin Luther King, Jr., sometimes children excitedly request a turn because they know they have tried something new! Also, amid all of the special reasons to share, Mrs. Harris keeps track of who shares to ensure that every child who wants to share does so within an approximate rotation. This is not a science; some children, for the special reasons mentioned above, may share more often than others.

Importantly, Mrs. Harris carefully teaches the children what to do when they share and what to do when they respond. This is vital! The share sessions must be meticulously orchestrated; if a turn in the Green Chair embarrasses a child, the child may instantly lose his excitement about writing. That possibility just cannot exist.

Mrs. Harris teaches them how to respond by using drafts she writes. The children find her creations fascinating when she tells about her drawings and reads her short texts to them. Her final words are, "What else would you like to know?" and they always have questions! Mrs. Harris loves to write about her old cat, and her drawings with sparse text beget many questions about his escapades.

When the children share she coaches them to do likewise. They tell about their drawings and read their print to the silent class on the carpet before them. Then they end their share with these final words, "What else would you like to know?" Before long, the children can share and respond without one single word from Mrs. Harris.

Then they are ready for another type of response. Over the course of the year she teaches them to ask, "What did you learn from my writing?" "What is interesting about my writing?" "What does my writing remind you of?" "What other writing does mine remind you of?"

And, depending on the situation—such as the day of Jamil's hats and the day of our Ron Mac snapshot—the class bursts into spontaneous applause. The response just comes. It is natural. They have much to say when their emotions are at a high point. "Why'd you write words?" "You wrote like we saw in the movie!" "It was in that book, too!" "Will you use purple tomorrow?" And Ron Mac answers the questions as they are asked.

The ultimate goals for the class share are for the writers to receive ideas for topics to write about, to gain ideas they may try as they intentionally grow as writers, and to stimulate and maintain their excitement about writing!

Overall, Mrs. Harris:

- shows respect for her students. She has established a classroom setting where they feel safe and willing to take chances.

- is patient. As an experienced teacher, she knows that not all children are ready to create writing they want to read to their class until several months have transpired. She allowed Ron Mac to move at his own pace.

- allows many different opportunities for the children in her classroom to interact and get to know each other on personal levels. This provides them with security.

Harrie and Roland's prekindergarten teacher created a new version of an all-class share.

On the first day of school, nine of Miss Robyn's fifteen children either did not speak English or English was their second language, and they were learning it.

During the first weeks Miss Robyn conducted an all-class share similar to that of Mrs. Harris, but the little four-year-old writers didn't respond much. Very few of them seemed to understand each other and/or talked to each other. This worried Miss Robyn—her children needed a great deal of oral language practice, but this setting produced quiet. As often as possible, they needed to be in situations where they were not quiet.

So, just as the children you have been reading about often try to figure out how to grow as writers, Miss Robyn tried to think of something to do differently as a writing teacher. One day it occurred to her to create the version of an all-class share you read about above. Instead of gathering around the Author's Chair, the children place their drafts on their tables and mill about, chatting, pointing, and exclaiming over each other's accomplishments.

And, importantly, their share time changed from one of quiet to a buzz of language!

Overall, Miss Robyn:

- has established a classroom routine where her diverse children are getting to know each other.

- realizes that children's pride in their work leads them to be self-confident writers.

- has created a classroom of excited four-year-old writers who wish to share with one another. Her children step into kindergarten as writers.

Writer-Friendly Classroom Features

Ron Mac's Kindergarten Classroom

As you may remember, the children in this class write on whatever topics they want four days a week, and on Fridays Mrs. Harris focuses her mini-lesson on a curricular area the class is studying. The children are to write about it.

Importantly, the snapshot of Ron Mac did not occur on a Friday. Ron Mac, on his own, decided to write about Martin Luther King, Jr. He, as happened with other children in Mrs. Harris's class, never wrote a personal narrative. In their writing workshop her young writers truly exercise topic choice. They write about anything they want—in any genre.

With the door wide open to welcome all their ideas, they all eventually enter the world of writers.

If you had been present when Ron Mac read his writing to his classmates, and they applauded, you may have found yourself tearing up. You may have sensed what they all knew. Not only are you in the midst of a class of children who value each other, you are in the presence of a young writer who has just stepped into the world of print.

And he figured out when and how to make his entry.

As an observer, you may think: This shatters everything I know about the development of young writers—and it does.

But it doesn't. When young writers enter Mrs, Harris's classroom from other cultures and languages, everything overwhelms them. She works hard to keep them surrounded with possibilities and encouragement.

None of us six authors has ever known a young writer who stayed outside the circle of writers for an entire year—and some of us have studied writers for decades. When children are in classrooms where they write (nearly) every day, talk while they write, share, and consistently receive supportive response/ evaluation from their classmates and teacher—they become writers.

For some, it is writing across the curriculum that pulls them in. They crave, need, and love the author-ity it provides them.

Harrie and Roland's Prekindergarten Classroom

If you were to walk into this prekindergarten classroom during one of their all-class shares, you would probably be impressed by the variety of writing. One type of writing chosen by a few children on any day is exemplified by Roland's depiction of *The Three Bears*.

Miss Robyn's prekindergarten class is part of the public school system, but it is also supported by federal funds, and all of her children live in families that experience financial concerns. Many of them, in addition, have not listened to children's literature throughout their young lives. Thus Miss Robyn reads to them more than once each day—and they love the books. She rereads many so they can chant along and memorize them. Plus, Miss Robyn provides time each day for the children to peruse books from their always-accessible classroom library, and they enjoy sitting on the carpet with their friends, reading and exclaiming over the happenings in the literature. Often, when they talk and read portions of the books, we hear the language of literature in their spoken words.

It is always a joy when children choose to write about one of the books. At a very early age they learn to use literature as mentor texts (Mermelstein, 2007), a practice they will continue throughout their lives as writers. All writers do this.

What This May Mean for Your Classroom

Some of you may be saying, "Given all the demands and standards, I just don't have time for my students to share with one another."

You will find that sharing takes such little time and, remember, standards of learning are taught "through the child's eyes." Children are natural teachers who have a lot of information to share about their families and about how to draw. Plus, they learn a lot about children's literature and about the curriculum they study. When they choose to write about those classroom experiences, the others learn from them when they share. Without hearing from the writers beyond the tables where they write, the children in your class will miss many learning opportunities.

Also, given the population of your class, you can be very creative! Sharing does not have to mean that everyone sits down on a carpet while one person shares their creations (although this can be a very effective way). Maybe you will find that having your writers move around to different tables works for them. Maybe you will create your own format for your children to use when they share. Importantly, as writing is a time for your students to be creative, you, the teacher, will have much flexibility in how you and your young writers share.

Some of you may be saying, "This sounds totally chaotic, with the children all wanting to share and wanting to hear about their classmates' writing."

Yes, it seems this may happen, but that will not necessarily be the case. Given that you will have created a classroom in which your children know you are fascinated by their writing, and you ask them every day to tell you about it, they copy your language. They want to know about each other's writing, and they ask. Plus, they are used to talking about their writing, so they tell. Because you are a supportive, interested teacher, you will have children who are supportive and interested.

When your children engage in these casual conversations about their writing they say a lot. Their oral language benefits—and they gather ideas for new things to try when they write. As the teacher, you will see their writing flourish with enthusiasm and zeal.

Finally, and very importantly, if you have children who are not too confident, by sharing their thoughts and ideas, your writers' self-esteem will grow and blossom.

Closing Thought

Children look forward to their all-class share as a time when they will hear their classmates' writing, see and hear ideas they may try in their writing, and offer their own thoughts in response. They often write with their classmates in mind, as all of the children in this chapter did. Ron Mac and Roland used shared experiences they knew their classmates were interested in—*The Three Bears* and the study of Martin Luther King, Jr.—as springboards to their writing. And Harrie wrote about a yucky personal experience—one he knew his friends would find fascinating! Young writers quickly learn which experiences will connect them to their classmates and will be quite likely to elicit especially engaging responses. After all, that's what sharing is about!

CHAPTER 9

We Honor Our Writers' Complete Lives

When we began to study young children as writers, our goal was to learn about what they did when they wrote across the curriculum. In hindsight, we now realize we started out with a huge misconception. We saw writing across the curriculum and writing about their lives as two separate areas of writing. Not so!

Yes, some children, such as Ron Mac (in the preceding chapter), love to write about their curricular studies, and choose to do so. Others are very willing to do so when we assign them. And they stay with a topic.

Importantly, however, what we learned is that many of the children do not separate their experiences outside of school from their experiences in school. One piece of writing often includes elements of their lives at school and elsewhere. In this book, you have seen this coming together of their worlds in the apples on the train tracks, in the movie Kasandra saw at home about civil rights concerns, and about the drought that entered the first-grade girl's essays about the world—of course their two worlds come together! That is the way we want their minds to work—and it took *their* writing for us to learn that writing across the curriculum includes *all* of the children's thinking. It's not surprising, given their enthusiastic embrace of new learning, that much of their writing and thinking arrives via "blended genres."

Snapshots of Braden and Charles

A First-Grade Writer and a Kindergarten Writer

We begin this final chapter with Braden—a first-grade writer who taught us much when we began our Writing Across the Curriculum (WAC) project. For the first days of school, the children wrote about whatever they wanted, and Elaine O'Connor learned about their families and other interests. Braden usually wrote about his love: monster trucks.

Then, excited about the possibilities of WAC, Ms. O'Connor, on the day of our snapshot, tells the children they will all write about their current unit of study: fall. They brainstorm ideas and go to their tables to write.

Braden remembers to write *Fall* in the upper left corner of his paper, and then creates his beloved monster trucks and two lines of print:

"I saw a monster truck.
The truck ran over cars."

While the children write, Ms. O'Connor walks among them, conferring. By the time she gets to Braden, he is just finishing his last line of print, and she asks him to read his writing to her. He does and immediately elaborates, "This one was the powerful one and it was . . . ." He continues on for a bit while Ms. O'Connor listens and then asks him about the little blue one. He spins yet another tale.

Then Ms. O'Connor says, "This is fascinating, Braden, but I'm remembering. I think we were going to write about fall today."

Almost before she can finish her sentence, Braden picks up an orange crayon and creates the leaves you see in his drawing. Fall!

For our second snapshot we feature Charles (the same Charles who turned a square into an adult in Chapter 1 and watched TV with his mom in Chapter 6) when he was in kindergarten, and taught us something similar to what we learned from Braden's monster trucks and orange leaves: Charles's at-home life reigned—even in the midst of the classroom curriculum.

It is spring, and Mrs. Harris's children are following their writing routine in which they write about whatever they want four days each week. Our snapshot occurs on Friday, the day the children write about their current unit of study, which is the life cycle of frogs. On the carpet, in their class cluster, they brainstorm ideas and then go to their tables to write.

Charles creates this life cycle:

"My tadpole went to the pond."

This is a bit difficult to decipher, but Charles starts on the lower left with his explanation, "The eggs. They kinda float around the lily pad." Then he moves farther up on the page. "The tadpole has a long tail and the tadpole's tail kinda goes away." The blurb on the right is, "The frog."

For his text, Charles initially wrote this part: *myiy ntoL W*

Then, he started over, and wrote the text he read: *m tAP w t D PON*.

Dorothy Suskind (the researcher in his classroom) and Charles talk about his excellent rendition of the eggs around the lily pad, and then she points to the two little shapes in the center, between the lily pad and the frog. "I'm wondering what these are, Charles."

"I lost two teeth last night!"

What These Writers Can Do: Strengths and Breakthroughs

- Both Braden and Charles create ways to integrate (or not quite!) the teacher's topic with their own lives. Their excitement about their lives takes over or springs into the task at hand. Braden is always into monster trucks and fall is just not quite that exciting, but he adds orange leaves. Charles has lost two teeth, and that is just way too important to ignore, even if this is a curriculum day.

- Charles can create a life cycle of a frog, a complicated kindergarten task. It is very important, we learned, to include opportunities for our young writers to engage in all types of writing across the curriculum, including diagrams. The children think they can do anything, and their efforts inform us about what they know.

Snapshots of Alexi

A Kindergarten Writer

It's easy to spot Alexi amid the bustle and chatter of Sue Harris's kindergarten classroom this morning. He's the one standing silently at his writing space, choosing two crayons from a box and placing them beside his writing book. Alexi usually plans for his writing and then organizes his space. He likes to know what he's going to write before he writes it. Alexi is quite deliberate, and not too chatty.

Alexi is an English language learner. Although born in the United States, his first language is Spanish. He speaks Spanish at home with his mother and father; English at home with his older brother. On this day, he demonstrates that he is adept not only at speaking in two languages in one space, but at writing in two languages as well.

With a shy grin on his face, Alexi says to researcher Jenesse Evertson, "I'm going to write in English *and* in Spanish today!" He is clearly pleased with this idea, and the Spanish words appear first, forming the title of his story. Then he writes a line of dialogue in English, and *Finished*—his version of *The End*.

*"One snake and dragon
Let's get ice cream
Finished"*

He gives his creation an appraising look, confidently picks up his writing, marches over to his teacher, and asks her if he can share from the Green Chair on this day. Mrs. Harris knows this must be an important piece for Alexi, who is usually economical with his spoken and written words. Most of the time, he places himself in situations where he is *not* the center of attention.

When it is Alexi's turn to share, he announces, "I'm going to read to you first in Spanish." He is preparing his audience for words they may not usually hear. When he finishes his Spanish/English reading, Marquis responds, "I like that you wrote Spanish *and* English." Alexi nods his head and gives another shy grin. He has discovered a space and place for writing in his two languages. The children ask him questions about his dragon and snake, and Alexi points out his dragon's forked tongue. The children express surprise that the two creatures are going for ice cream, and Alexi shines with another grin.

This snapshot happened in February, after Alexi had been writing in English all year, and after this initial exploration into writing in his first language, Alexi began to acknowledge his Spanish-speaking self in other ways, including short retellings/ rewritings of traditional tales from his Salvadoran culture or stories about his visits there.

Our next snapshot of Alexi happens in March. The draft he chooses to create provides him with the opportunity to consider the relationship between his language and his identity—a huge task for a young writer.

For a few days in the early part of March, Mrs. Harris has been writing a continuous story in her notebook for the class. Her story is about a giant who invades the school (such a frightfully appealing notion to five-year-olds!), and Alexi chooses to create his own version of the story.

In his version, a giant *troll* invades the school. Saving the children from impending doom is not the principal (too obvious!) of the school, but "Super Alexi." These are the easy decisions for this draft. But how will this small boy save the school? About this, Alexi is not quite sure.

Although Alexi usually comes to his writing time with a plan, today he asks his tablemates for help with this particular part of his draft. He has two ideas: Super Alexi can either 1) breathe fire at the troll, or 2) sing him to sleep with magic Spanish songs. When he poses his options to the children at his table, Kiersten responds, "Choose the English one!"

Alexi seems slightly puzzled by Kiersten's response. Is breathing fire the "English" choice? Hmmm . . . Instead of following her advice, Alexi chooses to have Super Alexi sing the magic Spanish songs, which he draws as notes floating in a stream from Super Alexi's mouth to the troll's ear:

"I throw magic Spanish songs. The troll falls asleep. Kasken School was safe today."

> **What This Writer Can Do: Strengths and Breakthroughs**
>
> - Alexi uses his writing to establish his Salvadoran identity. In this classroom where he is the only speaker of Spanish, it has taken him months to step forward and declare his identity in a public manner. He is different, and that is to be celebrated.
>
> - More specifically, Alexi knows that his identity as a Salvadoran enhances, rather than infringes upon, his membership in his classroom. Gradually, as many children have shared, he realizes that, in this classroom, all are honored, and he is no exception.
>
> - He knows his bilingual self makes him Super!

What the Teachers Do

Braden's first-grade teacher and Charles's kindergarten teacher created writing schedules that honor their desire for the children to write across the curriculum and the children's desire to write about their own interests.

Both teachers wanted to honor the children's need to write about their own interests, and the teachers also wanted the children to engage in Writing Across the Curriculum. In order for the children to do both, the two teachers created schedules that differed and worked for each of them.

Elaine O'Connor, first grade, adjusted by dividing the week into two days in which the children wrote about whatever they wanted—including curriculum areas, if they so chose—and two days in which the children wrote about a unit of study the class was engaged in at the time.

It did not take long for the children to adjust. They knew which days were which, and this worked well for them and for Ms. O'Connor.

Sue Harris, kindergarten teacher, set aside the first four days of each week for the children to write about whatever they chose. Then on Fridays they wrote about a unit of study the class had engaged in that week.

Alexi's kindergarten teacher reads and demonstrates many kinds of writing, set in various cultures.

The great diversity in Mrs. Harris's read-alouds and in her own daily writing help the children see the vast number of possibilities available in the world of writing.

She reads and writes personal narratives, fiction, poetry, and nonfiction. The children talk about the various topics and genres as ideas for their own writing and we see a wide variety in the classroom on any one day. Plus, their teachers hear the children's strong voices resound in their writing.

In addition, these two teachers:

- keep their students up to date on their own out-of-school lives, so the children become interested in their teachers' entire selves.

- engage in ongoing conversations with their young writers throughout the day. These conversations are about the children's lives beyond the school walls—and these chatty conversations are also about their studies. They know their students well, and the students know that math, social studies, or science can be a topic of conversation at any time.

- often set the curriculum lessons in settings the children experience in their out-of-school lives.

Writer-Friendly Classroom Features

Braden's First-Grade Classroom

If you had interacted with the children in Ms. O'Connor's classroom on the day Braden floated orange leaves over his monster trucks, you would have seen an active boy. While he writes, he sits on one knee, switches to the other, stands, and talks to everyone at his table. His classroom, where quiet talk is valued, assures his success. Braden talks and moves as fast as he threw those leaves into his illustration—and he does his work well.

You would have seen the other children write about fall in various ways. One girl drew four small pictures and wrote a sentence under each. Another child asked researcher Jane Hansen, "How do you spell *fall*? Not the kind like this, *when a pencil falls*, the kind like *It is fall*." Mrs. Hansen explained to the author that the two *falls* are spelled the same.

The children all wrote their own impressions of fall, in different genres, using illustrations in different ways, and placing their print in various places. In addition, they used their physical space and their classroom community in ways that suited them as writers. Braden may be a wiggler and a talker, and others may not. All children know there is space for them to work in the way that is best for them.

Alexi's Kindergarten Classroom

Today, with increasing numbers of English language learners in our classrooms, we six authors adapt to Spanish, Korean, African languages, more than one language from Burma, and others. We strive to honor diversity in a multitude of ways so the children learn to appreciate differences. To set up her classroom so variation thrives is Mrs. Harris's daily goal. Alexi meshed Mrs. Harris's ongoing story with cultural aspects of his own life and developed his unique piece of writing.

Mrs. Harris never quite knows what will make *the* difference for her young writers—the impetus to attempt something they have not yet considered. So Mrs. Harris tries many things, exploring the writing workshop from all angles. She asks: What do I do in my demonstrations? How do I arrange the room? How do I organize the time? She knows her young writers have much to explore in their busy school and home lives, and helping them to do so to the fullest extent requires them to examine and reexamine possibilities.

Importantly, Mrs. Harris knows that young writers, as real writers, wrestle with complex issues, including the ultimate: *Who am I?*

Undaunted, knowing they cannot do something wrong as a writer in this classroom, these children tackle the greatest of all unknowns. They enter the world of writing—as Alexi did—by flying straight in.

What This May Mean for Your Classroom

Some of you may be saying, "During writing time, I ask my students to write using story starters. I won't know what they know if I don't have all of them write about exactly the same thing."

Your children are sitting quietly at their desks as you hand each of them a lined piece of paper with the following prompt typed across the top of the page: "As I walked up the creaky stairs to the haunted house, all of a sudden I saw . . . ." Two of your children start writing immediately. We all have those two children. We thank goodness for those two children. Two of your children raise their hands to go to the bathroom, with no immediate plans to return. Who can blame those two children? The rest of your children look wide-eyed at you and the typical questions begin: How long does it have to be? Does spelling count? What do I write if I have never been to a haunted house?

Children really put us in our place. These questions actually yell the answers to our underlying concerns. Frederick asks how long the writing has to be, because to him this is an exercise in getting it done; it has nothing to do with him or his writing life. Trisha inquires if spelling counts, because she wants to know this assignment's formula for success, and it is clear to her that it is not about the power of the writing or the window into her writer's world. And leave it to Josh to state the obvious. Of course, he has never been to a haunted house; few of us have. Naturally, he could write fiction but, again, why a haunted house?

What you do in regularly distributing story starters is say: I am having you begin with these words, on a topic that you do not know about, and that you do not need to know about, because when you all complete the same story starter I can compare your abilities to put together a narrative that includes interesting experiences, an effective ending, correctly spelled words and proper punctuation. Go!

But if that is your goal, you can see these qualities and skills when Jorge writes about his father the firefighter, when Trisha tells about the baby bird she just nursed back to health, and when Josh explains the rules to the new video game his stepfather just gave him for his birthday.

Plus, you can assess children's writing when they write about the curriculum they are studying. You may ask your students to write about the life cycle of a bean plant or the ancient Egyptian pyramids. The children's options within the topic are open.

An important feature of the story starter provided about the haunted house is that you are asking the children to complete someone else's thoughts, and that limits their points of entry. By contrast, when a child writes about a self-selected topic or about a general topic within their studies, he is writing about a topic he knows. Plus, he is writing from his own perspective and, most important, he is writing to discover and learn. The learning is happening in the writing, on the spot. That is the power of it all.

So—should children ever write to story starters?

In your utopian world the answer would be a resounding NO! But even though NO is your preferred answer, you also understand that your students are required to write to a story starter or a more general prompt on your state and school division tests, and those scores are tied to school funding and grade promotion. Since this is a requirement, you will provide your students with practice. That is only fair. You will teach them ways to approach test situations, just like you teach them how to properly fill out a test bubble with a No. 2 pencil. But you call that writing instruction for test practice.

Writing instruction is when you teach your students what to do so they become excited about themselves as writers! So, much as you do as a reader when you can't wait to get back into a book, your young writers want to get back into *their* writing.

You teach them the many options to consider when work on their self-selected or content specific topics from their own perspective and experiences—and they learn as they write. That is writing across the curriculum.

Some of you may be saying, "I tell my students they cannot include personal information in their content writing."

Children's worlds are rich. They notice things. As one of your students finishes sorting his word study words, he notices the dead fly in the corner. Later, during writing workshop, he creates a story around that fly. On her way to school this morning, one of the girls in your class saw a biker get run off the road. It is 9:00 a.m. and she has already relayed the story to her teacher, the reading specialist, and the school secretary. And when it's time for lunch, you predict she will tell the lunch lady.

Your children do not put boundaries on their lives or their writing. They experience breakfast with their grandmas, morning commutes with their older brother, read-alouds with you, and recess time with their friends, and roll it all together into one big ball they call their life. Your young writers' experiences, like your experiences, shape how they interpret and connect to the curriculum.

As you read this book, you read it through the lens of your own experiences in the classroom. As you work on a fictional narrative, your mischievous main character probably reflects one of your own sons. When you write your weekly newsletter home to the parents, you write it through your eyes. It would probably be different if the students wrote it.

Your children are doing the same thing. Thank goodness they are. You want to know their take, their flair, and how their lives intertwine with classroom topics. When a kindergarten child drops his lost tooth right in the middle of his frog's life cycle and when another child writes in dual languages, they are doing something profound.

These children are yelling to us, to you, their teacher, "Hey, this is my education and my curriculum, and I am working hard to connect what you are teaching me to what I am learning in my larger world." And isn't that one of our/your main educational goals? To connect the curriculum to the lives of your children? To make it relevant? How brilliant that our young children do this naturally.

The young children we studied and the young children in your classroom set the standard they hope we will follow.

Some of you may be saying, "We write personal narratives in writing workshop and explore curriculum areas in writing during social studies and science time."

We started this way, too. Traditionally, writing workshop was when children wrote creatively about their own life and experiences. But once again, our students set us straight. During writing workshop time our children instinctively write about how the eagles in Virginia flap their wings "up and down and down and up," just like the ones in their study of desert life.

Our children and yours do not naturally and neatly separate their writing lives into units of study. We/you do that. But something magical happens when you stop compartmentalizing children's writing time; they write across the curriculum (their curriculum) in writing workshop.

As your students write, they also talk. So now, instead of having every child complete an "All About Me" book using a prescribed format, your children are writing about diverse topics, expanding their understandings through conversations as they write, and including themselves whenever they want—in all kinds of writing. In your classroom writing workshop is a bustling of voices. Kendra asks Mary, "What size was the bean seed again?" and Jack questions Beliz, "How many stripes does the American flag have?"

All of a sudden, you have content bouncing back and forth among the classroom tables and up and down off the classroom walls, as the knowledge of your students grows. In your classroom, writing workshop becomes the space where children not only grow as writers but blossom as scientists, historians, and mathematicians. This type of environment prepares them for middle school, high school, and professional writing lives—where the majority of their writing is in response to content. And it's all very much in keeping with the new Common Core Standards and 21st-Century Learning Skills that call for collaborative problem solving and inquiry (Trilling & Fadel, 2009).

Now, not all of your children will choose to write about content during writing time. That is fine. Much of the power of a workshop grows from different voices pursuing diverse avenues of expression. This is what opens doors in the classroom and allows children to enter the lives of their classmates.

You may decide to let your children write on topics of their choice every day during writing workshop time, or you may decide to follow the lead of Elaine or Sue and designate one or two writing workshop days per week to content writing, though many kids will designate additional days on their own. However you choose to organize your writing week, your class writing days will be powerful. The children will learn about the topics they purse as they write, they will highlight misunderstandings for you to address, and they will expand the knowledge of their classmates through investigative talk.

On these content days, you might say, "We have been learning about the life cycle of frogs, and today I would like for you to use your writing as a way to explore some of the things you have learned." This is very different from giving a child a premade book that requires her to complete a sentence on each page and draw a corresponding picture. In your classroom, one child might draw a diagram of the parts of a frog, another child might tell a narrative story about how Mary the tadpole grew into a frog, and another child might draw four boxes and show how the life cycle of a frog progresses over time. Through table talk the children will learn about each other's take on the topic and that sharing will be expanded as a few children read their writing aloud to the class before they head to recess.

Writing workshop in your classroom is a playground of possibilities—where young writers explore their lives, their friendships, and what they are learning in school. Importantly, they do so in combinations that no units of study could have planned, because their writing authentically grows out of your unique classroom and the individual connections made by YOUR young writers.

Closing Thought

For this, our final closing thought, we end with the words of one of the children—Cassie, the kindergarten girl you met in Chapter 7, the one who eventually created a "Beautiful Tree."

Several weeks after she created her tree, a new student joined their classroom and, as was the case with most of the new students, she came from a classroom where she had not become a writer. Mrs. Harris asked Cassie to be the new girl's mentor. Sitting beside her during their writing workshop, Cassie couldn't help but notice what researcher Jenesse Evertson did: This new student didn't know where to begin. You could almost see a cloud of confusion surrounding her. So, Cassie offered her some advice:

Let me tell you
what you can write about

A jack-in-the-box
A milkshake
A dog
A bird

Do you know
how to make
dogs and birds?

Can you make
a little "h"?
I can.
Like this.
(Cassie finger-draws in the air.)

Can you make
a little "I"?
I can.
Like this.
(Cassie finger-draws in the air.)

Can you make
a square?
I can.
Like this.
(Cassie finger-draws in the air.)

You can write like me
Or
You can write
Anything
You want.

It's writing time.
That's what you do.

REFERENCES

Allen, Camille, & Swistak, Laurie (2004). Multigenre research: The power of choice and interpretation. *Language Arts, 81*(3), 223–232.

Bricker, Patricia (2007). Reinvigorating science journals. *Science and Children,* November, 24–29.

Calkins, Lucy, Hartman, Amanda, & White, Zoe (2005). *One to one: The art of conferring with young writers.* Portsmouth, NH: Heinemann.

Campano, Gerald, Leland, Christine, & Harste, Jerome C. (2004). Curriculum as identity: Writing the word, writing the world. *Talking Points, 38*(1), 38–39.

Cappello, Marva (2006). Under construction: Voice and identity development in writing workshop. *Language Arts, 83*(6), 482–491.

Cazden, Courtney (2001). *Classroom discourse: The language of teaching and learning.* Portsmouth, NH: Heinemann.

Donovan, Maggie, & Sutter, Cheryl (2004). Encouraging doubt and dialogue: Documentation as a tool for critique. *Language Arts, 81*(5), 377–384.

Dorfman, Lynn, & Cappelli, Rose (2009). *Nonfiction mentor texts: Teaching information writing through children's literature, K–8.* Portland, ME: Stenhouse.

Dorfman, Lynn, & Cappelli, Rose (2007). *Mentor texts: Teaching writing through children's literature, K–6.* Portland, ME: Stenhouse.

Dudley-Marling, Curt, & Searle, Dennis (1991). *When students have time to talk: Creating contexts for learning language.* Portsmouth, NH: Heinemann.

Dyson, Anne Haas (2003). *The brothers and sisters learn to write: Popular literacies in childhood and school cultures*. New York: Teachers College Press.

Edelsky, Carole, Smith, Karen, & Faltis, Christian (2008). *Side-by-side learning: Exemplary literacy practices for English language learners and English speakers in the mainstream classroom*. New York: Scholastic.

Fay, Kathleen, & Whaley, Suzanne (2004). *Becoming one community: Reading and writing with English Language Learners*. York, ME: Stenhouse.

Fletcher, Ralph, & Portalupi, JoAnn (2001). *Writing workshop: The essential guide*. Portsmouth, NH: Heinemann.

Gallas, Karen (2003). *Imagination and literacy: A teacher's search for the heart of learning*. New York: Teachers College Press.

Genishi, C., Stires, S.E., & Yung-Chan, D. (2001). Writing in an integrated curriculum: Prekindergarten English language learners as symbol makers. *Elementary School Journal, 101,* 399–416.

Glover, Matt (2009). *Engaging young writers: Preschool–grade 1*. Portsmouth, NH: Heinemann.

Graves, Donald (2003). *Writing: Teachers and children at work* (20th anniversary edition). Portsmouth, NH: Heinemann.

Graves, Donald, & Hansen, Jane (1984). The Author's Chair. *Language Arts, 60*(2), 176–187.

Hahn, Mary Lee (2002). *Reconsidering read-aloud*. York, ME: Stenhouse.

Hansen, Jane (2005). Young children's versions of the curriculum: "How do you turn a square into a grown-up?" *Language Arts, 82*(5), 269–277.

Hansen, Jane (2007a). First-grade children revisit their writing. *Young Children, 62*(1), 28–33.

Hansen, Jane (2007b). Teachers' and researchers' uses of assessment and evaluation can bring reading and writing together. *The Canadian Journal of Program Evaluation, 22*(3), 1–28.

Hansen, Jane (2009). Young writers use mentor texts. In D. A. Wooten & B. E. Cullinan (Eds.), *Children's literature in the reading program: An invitation to read* (p. 88–98). Newark, DE: International Reading Association.

Heard, Georgia, & McDonough, Jennifer (2009). *A place for wonder: Reading and writing nonfiction in the primary grades.* York, ME: Stenhouse.

Heard, Georgia. (2002). *The revision toolbox: Teaching techniques that work.* Portsmouth, NH: Heinemann.

Henry, Marguerite (1947/1975). *Misty of Chincoteague.* New York: Scholastic.

Heuser, Daniel (2002). *Reworking the workshop: Math and science reform in the primary grades.* Portsmouth, NH: Heinemann.

Hindley, Joanne (1996). *In the company of children.* Portland, ME: Stenhouse.

Horn, Martha, & Giacobbe, Mary Ellen (2007). *Talking, drawing, writing: Lessons for our youngest writers.* Portland, ME: Stenhouse.

Hubbard, Ruth Shagoury, & Shorey, Virginia (2003). Worlds beneath the words: Writing workshop with second language learners. *Language Arts, 81*, 52–61.

Johnston, Peter (2004). *Choice words: How our language affects children's learning.* Portland, ME: Stenhouse.

Jones, Stephanie (2004). Living poverty and literacy learning: Sanctioning topics of students' lives. *Language Arts, 81*(6), 461–469.

Kissel, Brian (2009). Beyond the page: Peers influence pre-kindergarten writing through talk, image, and movement. *Childhood Education, 85*(3), 160–166.

Kissel, Brian (2008a). Apples on train tracks: Observing young children reenvision their writing. *Young Children*, March, 26–32.

Kissel, Brian (2008b). Promoting writing and preventing writing failure in young children. *Preventing School Failure, 52*(4), 53–56.

Kissel, Brian, & Baker, Marianne (2008). The role of informational text in the writing of pre-kindergarten children. *Balanced Reading Instruction*, 75–89.

Laminack, Lester, & Wadsworth, Reba M. (2006a). *Learning under the influence of language and literature: Making the most of read-alouds across the day.* Portsmouth, NH: Heinemann.

Laminack, Lester L., & Wadsworth, Reba M. (2006b). *Reading aloud across the curriculum: How to build bridges in language arts, math, science, and social studies.* Portsmouth, NH: Heinemann.

Lawrence, Jody (2006). Revoicing: How one teacher's language creates active learners in a constructivist classroom. *The Constructivist.* Retrieved from www.odu.edu/educ/act/journal/vol17no1/

Lensmire, Timothy (1997). *Powerful writing, responsible teaching.* New York: Teachers College Press.

Lewison, Mitzi, Leland, Christine, & Harste, Jerome (2007). *Creating critical classrooms: K–8 Reading and writing with an edge.* New York: Routledge.

Lindfors, Judith (2008). *Children's language: Connecting reading, writing, and talk.* New York: Teachers College Press.

Madigan, Dan, & Koivu-Rybicki, Victoria (1997). *The writing lives of children.* York, ME: Stenhouse.

Marcus, Leonard S. (2002). Interview with Ashley Bryan. In *Ways of telling: Conversations on the art of the picture book* (pp. 18–31). New York: Dutton Children's Books.

Mermelstein, Leah (2007). *Don't forget to share: The crucial last step in the writing workshop.* Portsmouth, NH: Heinemann.

Moss, Barbara (2005). Making a case and a place for effective content area literacy instruction in the elementary grades. *The Reading Teacher, 59*(1), 46–55.

Murray, Donald (1999). *Write to learn.* Fort Worth: Harcourt Brace College Publishers.

National Commission on Writing in America's Schools and Colleges (2003). *The neglected "R": The need for a writing revolution.* College Entrance Examination Board. Retrieved from www.collegeboard.com

Newkirk, Thomas (2009). *Holding on to good ideas in a time of bad ones.* Portsmouth, NH: Heinemann.

Newkirk, Thomas (2007). Popular culture and writing development. *Language Arts, 84*(6), 539–548.

Newkirk, Thomas (2002). *Misreading masculinity: Boys, literacy, and popular culture.* Portsmouth, NH: Heinemann.

Nieto, Sonia (2002). *Language, culture, and teaching: Critical perspectives for a new century.* Mahwah, NJ: Erlbaum.

Norton, Nadjwa Effat Laila (2005). Permitanme hablar: Allow me to speak. *Language Arts, 83*(2), 118–127.

Nye, Naomi Shihab (2005). Spiral staircase. *The Horn Book Magazine, 81*(3), 251–254.

Ostrow, Jill (1999). *Making problems, creating solutions: Challenging young mathematicians.* York, ME: Stenhouse.

Paley, Vivian Gussin (2004). *A child's work: The importance of fantasy play.* Chicago: The University of Chicago Press.

Pransky, Ken (2008). *Beneath the surface: The hidden realities of teaching culturally and linguistically diverse young learners K–6.* Portsmouth, NH: Heinemann.

Ray, Katie Wood, with Lisa B. Cleaveland (2004). *About the authors: Writing workshop with our youngest writers.* Portsmouth, NH: Heinemann.

Ray, Katie Wood, & Glover, Matt (2008). *Already ready: Nurturing writers in preschool and kindergarten.* Portsmouth, NH: Heinemann.

Ray, Katie Wood (2001). *The writing workshop: Working through the hard parts (and they're all hard parts).* Urbana, IL: National Council of Teachers of English.

Read, Sylvia (2005). First and second graders writing informational text. *The Reading Teacher, 59*(1), 36–44.

Reardon, Jeanne (2002). Writing: A way into thinking science. In Wendy Saul, Jeanne Reardon, Charles Pearce, Donna Dieckman, & Donna Neutze, *Science workshop: Reading, writing, and thinking like a scientist* (pp. 86–100). Portsmouth, NH: Heinemann.

Rogovin, Paula (2001). *The research workshop: Bringing the world into your classroom.* Portsmouth, NH: Heinemann.

Rosenblatt, Louise (2005). *Making meaning with texts: Selected essays.* Portsmouth, NH: Heinemann.

Saul, Wendy, Reardon, Jeanne, Pearce, Charles, Dieckman, Donna, & Neutze, Donna (2002). *Science workshop: Reading, writing, and thinking like a scientist.* Portsmouth, NH: Heinemann.

Shagoury, Ruth (2009). *Raising writers: Understanding and nurturing young children's writing development.* Boston: Pearson Education.

Sherrill, Carl (2005). Math riddles: Helping children connect words and numbers. *Teaching Children Mathematics, 11*(7), 368–375.

Solley, Bobbie A. (2005). *When poverty's children write: Celebrating strengths, transforming lives.* Portsmouth, NH: Heinemann.

Stone, Jennifer (2005). Textual borderlands: Students' recontextualizations in writing children's books, *Language Arts, 83*(1), 42–51.

Sumida, Anna, & Meyer, Meleanna (2006). Teaching to the fourth power: Transformative inquiry and the stirring of cultural waters. *Language Arts, 83*(5), 437–449.

Suskind, Dorothy (2007). Curriculum makers: Children use their critical stories to construct understanding. *Talking Points, 18*(2), 11–16.

Trilling, Bernie, & Fadel, Charles (2009). *21st-century skills: Learning for life in our times.* San Francisco, CA.: Jossey-Bass.

Van Leeuwen, Charlene, & Gabriel, Martha (2007). Beginning to write with word processing: Integrating writing process and technology in a primary classroom. *The Reading Teacher, 60*(5), 420–429.

Van Sluys, Katie (2003). Writing and identity construction: A young author's life in transition. *Language Arts, 80*, 176–184.

Vasquez, Vivian (2003). What if and why? Critical literacy, children's literature, and mathematics investigations. In *Getting beyond "I like the book": Creating space for critical literacy in K–6 classrooms* (pp. 67–80). Newark, DE: International Reading Association.

Whitin, Phyllis (2007). The ties that bind: Emergent literacy and scientific inquiry. *Language Arts, 85*(1), 20–30.

Wilson, Maja (2006). *Rethinking rubrics in writing assessment*. Portsmouth, NH: Heinemann.

Wiseman, Angela, M. (2003). Collaboration, initiation, and rejection: The social construction of stories in a kindergarten class. *The Reading Teacher, 58*, 802–810.

Wynne-Jones, Tim (2002). Where ideas really come from. *The Horn Book Magazine*, September/October, 625–629.

ABOUT THE AUTHORS

Robyn Davis

Robyn has taught for fourteen years and has held various primary-level teaching responsibilities. For the last several years Robyn has taught prekindergarten in the Charlottesville City Schools, Charlottesville, Virginia. Robyn is the mother of two daughters and is a lifelong resident of Charlottesville.

Jenesse Evertson

Jenesse has a doctoral degree from the University of Virginia and was an elementary classroom and literacy teacher for eight years in various states. Since we started this book, Jenesse has become the mother of two children who keep her busy in Europe, currently in England.

Tena Freeman

Tena has taught for many years, the last several at her present school, St. Andrews, in Richmond, Virginia. She loves the close atmosphere of this special little school. Tena enjoys spending time with her grandchildren, and she and her husband enjoy weekend trips on their Harleys.

Jane Hansen

Jane is a professor at the University of Virginia, where she focuses on the teaching of writing and conducting research on writers of various ages. In addition, she directs the Central Virginia Writing Project. Jane and her husband love the outdoors, music, and travels to their origins in the Midwest.

Dorothy Suskind

Dorothy teaches fifth grade at St. Christopher's School in Richmond and has held other elementary teaching positions. In addition, she was a professor at the University of Mary Washington, Fredericksburg, Virginia. Dorothy has two sons and is a lifelong resident of Richmond, Virginia.

Holly Tower

Holly is a professor at Lewis-Clark State College in Lewiston, Idaho, a position and location she greatly enjoys. Previously, she was an elementary literacy teacher and a secondary special education teacher is school divisions in Virginia. Holly loves to share the escapades of her two sons.